this is a love song

Thoughts from the B Side of a Gen X Life

dina honour

SCYLLA

PRESS

Published by Scylla Press, USA

Cover design: Karen Honour

ISBN/Print: 979-8-9891100-2-5

ISBN/Digital: 979-8-9891100-3-2

To the athletes, the criminals, the brains, the princesses, and the basket cases—but especially to Diane, Joanne, and Kelly, who not only shared their Aqua Net with me but also four decades of spinach dip, wine, and friendship.

contents

also by

It's a lot to Unpack

There's Some Place Like Home: Lessons from a Decade Abroad

composition notes

Oh, nostalgia, that wistful yearning for days of yore, when everything appears quaint and ye olde. Nostalgia adds a layer of padding, a buffer between the here and now, between the way things are and the way they *used to be*. Sometimes, the past feels safer, like a security blanket we can hunker down into. When the outside world gets too loud or scary, it feels good to retreat into those sepia-tinted memories where things seem quaint. The *before times* are comfortable—we're familiar with the roads that take us through the past, we recognize the rest stops, and we know where to stop to fill our tanks when we're running low.

It's easy, then, to start to make comparisons. Which times were better? When were things easier, less complicated, or more fulfilling?

Nothing in this book is meant as a comparison. I've no desire to get dragged into a generational tug-of-war, digging in my heels on a mashed potato mountain by insisting that close encounters of any kind were better or harder back in my day. Nothing is meant as an intentional dig at the generations that came before or have followed.

There's plenty of that on social media.

Some of the work that appears here was first published or republished on various blogs or social media platforms. Unless otherwise stated, the experiences and thoughts expressed throughout are my own. Older work has been updated to reflect current thinking, and some names have been changed to protect privacy or people who have no idea they live rent-free in my head.

Finally, it's important to acknowledge that I'm writing from a place of privilege. I'm a college-educated White woman with a financial safety net. Those things have shaped my experiences, both then and now. It would be silly and arrogant to assume that everyone shares my views or experiences just because they were born between a set of bookended years that arbitrarily define a generation.

Goonies might never say die, but we all walk through life in different shoes.

These are mine.

prelude

The B Side

I was born in 1970.

It was the year The Beatles finally called it quits, and Apollo 13 called Houston with a problem. Both Jimi Hendrix and Janis Joplin overdosed and cemented their legacy in the infamous 27 Club. The Jackson Five debuted on television, several countries declared independence from Great Britain, the war in Vietnam was ongoing, and there was too much global political unrest to list. The times, they were a-changin', though probably not fast enough.

1970 puts me closer to early Generation X, the great question mark of a cohort that no one knew what to do with.

They still don't—when they remember us, that is.

It also means I was among the lucky Xers to turn fifty smack in the middle of 2020, the year of the great plague. In a strange way, hitting the half-century mark during lockdown was a relief. The pressure to dig out the sequins and pop champagne into the wee hours was lifted, courtesy of a fast-spreading virus and government restrictions. I could sit at home in my elasticated pants, drinking rosé and eating pizza.

For me, the milestone birthdays that end with zeros are never as fraught as the years before, the ones that end with nines. Those are my countdown years, 365 days of sorting out my mental clutter to determine if I'm ready to enter into the next decade reasonably intact—or if it's going to be a hot mess kind of era. It's an even split. The "nine" years are usually full of reflection and endless lists of things I've done, haven't done, or wake up at two am regretting for either reason.

By the time the big zero day rolls around, it often feels anti-climactic.

Still...fifty is a big number no matter which way you look at it, and I looked at it from all angles, mostly trying to make sense of how I got there.

Fifty is the last of the big potential halfway birthdays. 100 is unlikely, sure, but it's *possible*. No one is living until 120, not even the weirdos who have had their heads cryogenically frozen. Fifty, though, felt heavy, like a birthday that was weighted down with cinder blocks of meaning.

Fifty was screaming, *"You can't avoid me. Look, look, look!"*

I *was* looking. I was looking as it barreled toward me at speed. I was looking for a hiding space, but there was nothing I could do to stop that number from hitting me head-on.

So I did what I do best—I wrote a lot of words.

Throughout 2020 and into 2021, I kept a series of journals, writing in longhand, though not nearly as neatly as the penmanship I perfected way back in Mrs. Vacca's third-grade class. The journals were a way to keep sane during Covid, but also a way to document the ramp-up—and then the aftermath—to the big, scary birthday. Maybe if I peered through the pages I was writing or peeled back the skin of those sentences, I could grasp onto something to make it less frightening. Or so I hoped.

The birthday came and went. Cake was eaten, champagne was drunk, and video calls came in from friends scattered around the world. The pandemic rose, fell, and then rose again. The notebooks where I had scribbled my thoughts got packed and moved across the border from Denmark to Germany. They sat on my desk, pushed to the side while I worked on *It's a Lot to Unpack*. Another birthday came, and then another.

Until finally, I took the notebooks out again.

Buried in those handwritten pages were my hopes and fears, lessons, and questions. There were messy feelings about aging, my body, my marriage and kids, the world around me, and how all of those things had changed or were changing. There was a lot of nonsense and a lot of feeling sorry for myself, but there were also seedlings that bloomed into many of the essays that appear in this collection.

When I was a child, it seemed like the days and years stretched forever in front of me, as endless as the stars. Then, in a blink, I was traversing high school hallways, then college campuses, then office cubicles. Time sped up. Life happened. People loved, and people died. People married and divorced. Kids were born, grew up, and some started having children of their own.

It all went by so fast, just like they said it would—those old, cranky people who liked to talk about things *back in the day*.

Despite my best efforts at stopping the clock, I am now the cranky old person who likes to write about things *back in the day*.

What's life like here, on the flip side of the half-century mark? On the B side? Like the vinyl records we used to collect, got rid of, and are now buying again at double the cost, things are a little scratchy. Sometimes my brain skips. Like my beloved mixtapes, things jam and freeze, and I've got to spend a stupid amount of time fiddling to make them work again. Sometimes, it feels like I've forgotten a part of myself, only to come across the missing piece in a flea market bin or in the pocket of a vintage coat in a second-hand shop—one I've probably owned before.

I can't go back and remaster the first five decades of my life.

What I *can* do, though, is rewind and listen again. Things always sound different the second or third time around, when you hear more than just the hit songs and the high notes, when you've lived a lot more life, and the lyrics start to take on a different meaning.

<u>Joan Collins</u>

...put my glasses on. And then I look ok and then I take them off again. I think Mother Nature is post-menopausal herself because right about the time the wrinkles and neck sag really start to appear, your eye-sight goes as well and it's a bit like living in a perma-Joan Collins sort of er mode. Which is good- great even - except n you see a photograph and think who ...ell is that turkey-necked woman standing

...se of priv...

...ll of motherhood.

...d, it's weird, but its there.

...y crushes on boys. Craig

...h his yellow blonde hair and

...ll jacket, the unrecognizable

...p in my stomach whenever h

...the irrational jealousy of Max

...d". There was an endless st

...ndy, David - jock names, bo

...heart would flutter and I would

...ssly, against the wall of the high

...r the movie-ending. It raveli

paying attention to you do
- they do is to think "she looks good...
own an behave and never
to" just to have the
so a g" tacked on. Bullshit

we all pilates and run and

Why can't we... why can't we kick and scream? ...to age
and aches and pains of aging? Why is it
so binary? ...both the wisdom

No one tells you things. You find yourself
huddled in a corner (menopause whisperer)
worrying there is a faint whiff of moth
balls coming off your skin like some crone
perfume they sell at Nordström's. Eau du
crone or something. And it's all

2/11/21

I'm pretty sure I thought I was too good
for Dolly Parton. I'm pretty sure I thought I
was too punk rock, too "I-" eminist, too cool for
Appalachia school. Of course suddenly you turn
50 and even though you might know you are
deeply cool, no one else does. Or at least no one
between the ages of 15 and 49. So maybe you
start to revisit some things in the past. Maybe
you have a husband with a deep and un-
conditional love for Islands in the Stream. Who
Dolly Parton is... well,

thoughts from the
b side of a gen x life

she let herself go

. . .

During Covid, my husband and I walked daily. It was a way to escape the claustrophobia of boredom, of our apartment, and of the pandemic itself. Walking was an attempt to ground ourselves in whatever small bit of normalcy we could find. Something about moving your body moves your mind, and so those walks also became the way we tried to make sense of the topsy-turvy times we were living in.

Even now, there are times I look back and think, *Did that really happen? Was it all just a collective Bobby Ewing dream sequence?*

Now that life is back to something like normal, our walks have become less frequent: Saturday morning strolls to a farmer's market, an after-dinner amble on a balmy evening, and sometimes, a fast-paced Thursday stomp along the pavement as a way to tame some new anxiety that's cropped up. There always seem to be new anxieties cropping up.

Our walking conversations veer wildly, from politics to generational denim wars to whether or not we should bother trying to figure out what *skibidi* means. Once, while we were tromping through the Danish woods, sneakers squelching in the spring mud, we ended up talking about bras.

My husband, with the innocence of someone who has never experienced the pleasure of whipping off a bra at the tail end of a day, asked me, "Why do you even wear a bra?"

I looked at him in confusion. I sputtered something about low-hanging fruit and a fear of looking my age—and how, of course, I know it's all cosmetic and vain—and on and on. Meanwhile, as I was spouting the party line to the breast of my ability, my thoughts whirred like a bingo cage.

I wear a bra—and do a whole bunch of other things—because I don't want people to look at me and think, "She's *let herself go.*"

She let herself go. Oh, the horror of it.

She let herself go. What does it even mean? She had the audacity to age? To gain weight? To let a crown of silver and gray shine through? We're a century removed from corsets and a few more from foot binding, but we are still hobbling ourselves, forcing our bodies and minds into uncomfortable garments and unrealistic ideals, bending and twisting to fit into tiny boxes that were never meant to hold us.

Maybe the restraints aren't as physical as a whalebone corset or ribbons of cloth wound like a tourniquet around your toes, but the effects are essentially the same. The girdles are just psychological now.

Women often declare that we want to age *gracefully*, like a ballet dancer pirouetting around the years, limber and lithe. I've said it myself. Not for me the fillers and the botulism in a bottle! Not for me, the ragged clawing to the last vestiges of youth! I shall age gracefully, a long-necked swan of the middle years.

Of course, it's much easier to declare such things when you are twenty or thirty or even forty and things are still held in place with gravity and not Spanx, when there is an abundance of collagen and oceans of estrogen, and when Mother Nature's idea of a midlife joke hasn't yet wreaked havoc on your body and psyche. And then, one day, you're downward-facing like a dog, and you notice the way the skin on the front of your thighs just...sags. Like sad clowns. And so you march in place, ever faster, determined not to be one of those women we whisper about, one of those women who *let herself go*.

Go where? I wonder. Go wherever it is your body is going to take you, into the future? Go into the aftermorrow with your increasingly creaky knees and your ankles that twinge when you step onto the bedroom floor in the early morning?

So much time we spend chasing our past selves, trying to catch them in the cup of our palms like a sunbeam. Oh, I do it too, peeking through the net of my fingers to see if there's a sliver of youth there, as if somehow, if only I can figure out how to trap it, I can use it as a balm to soften the fine lines around my mouth.

SHE LET HERSELF GO. Have you seen her?

I think she's put on weight; she's definitely put on weight. She *put it on*. Like a suit she can take off and hang carefully in the closet among the just-in-case dresses and the ones that no longer fit but maybe could one day if she just tried harder. Just a little bit harder. She put it on. It's bought and paid for, and the receipt was thrown out a decade ago. Or—maybe she stopped starving herself, maybe she grew tired of turning down the birthday cake, or maybe she added up the money and time and effort on a calculator she keeps for such things—the cost of trying to convince her bones that they needed to bend into a shape they were never meant to be in.

SHE LET HERSELF GO. Have you seen her?

She's not even making an effort. No, she is not even trying.

As if effort is defined by certain fabrics, ones with spandex or technical fibers that suffocate your internal organs. As if trying only counts if the cut of the bias is restrictive or the heel height is hobbling. Or—maybe she grew tired of the way the waistband of her jeans was garroting her stomach, leaving marks like bruises, or how her tendons were shortened from years of office heels, or the effort it took to look glossy and kempt just to retrieve the mail from the end of the drive.

SHE LET HERSELF GO. *Have you seen her?*

She looks tired, haggard even. She doesn't seem to care. As if caring is measured in the brightness of a concealer stick or contoured jowl. As if caring only counts if it works to mask the truth behind pancake makeup and the blush of faux youth. Or—maybe she isn't sleeping because she's caught in a hormonal vortex or her kids are growing up, but so are her parents, and she's stuck in the middle, spinning her wheels, staring at a white ceiling in the dark part of night, plum-tinted skin under her eyes in the morn.

SHE LET HERSELF GO. *Have you seen her?*

She looks *old*. Like an old woman. As if she didn't use the right creams or potions, witches' brews lined up in pretty jars on her shelf. As if she doesn't care that by looking old, she is forcing us to confront the passage of time. As if it's too much to ask to use the face rollers and gua shas and prick the delicate skin under her eyes with thin needles to not look so... on the way to old. On the way to old because *true old* is acceptable. True old is safe. We squeal and titter over truly old women because we've stripped them of their power, and their brittle bones pose no threat. But aging on the way to old? Well, that is simply too much. There is too much raw energy, too much bare anger and rage. Too many feelings worn on the outside, showing, demanding we look. It's too confrontational.

She let herself go.

I'M NOT IMMUNE, not at all. I still squeeze myself into corsets of expectation. I want to look good for my age; I have bought the weighted vest, and the witches' jars on my shelf catch the morning light. I have surreptitiously picked up the brochures at the dermatologist's and made polite inquiries.

I don't want to let myself go, you know?

Until that day in the damp, Danish wood, I had never stopped to consider the unspoken part of the phrase. "To go" implies movement; it implies direction.

Where do you go when you let yourself go?

What if we've been wrong all this time? What if the *"where"* is not to pasture or to seed but somewhere else altogether? What if it's freedom, like a balloon let loose from a tight, sticky grip, caught on the breeze, tripping over telephone wires into the clouds? What if it's on an adventure, a journey to the center of yourself? What if it's a release from a grip that has always been too tight?

What if you let yourself go, and on the way, you become the wise woman, the witch, the crone, the elder from the books and movies who outsmarts us all because she eats the truth for breakfast, spitting out the bones?

What if, when you let yourself go, you'd actually be going *somewhere*?

She let herself go. Have you seen her?

She's flying free.

a marriage story

. . .

Once upon a time, on a late New York City afternoon, there was an itty-bitty slip of a thing—or as itty-bitty as a 5'9", thirty-year-old woman could be. She was so teeny that she wasn't even wearing a bra, and there was no jiggling or jangling. It truly was a miracle on 14th Street. There was a prince of a man in a morning suit, and there were yummy cupcakes and wheatgrass in boxes in the center of the tables, a single, pink orchid in each—because it was the early noughties and that sort of thing was hip and cool.

There was food and drink and merriment. There was song and dance and borrowed words by Jeanette Winterson and e.e. cummings. There were things she remembered and things she forgot, and somewhere, in the space between the two, there was a duo of *I dos*.

Now, of course, I am no longer thirty or an itty bitty slip of a thing. There is a lot more jiggling and jangling. I remember even less and forget even more of that day, only jigsaw pieces that occasionally fit together in a pattern. I remember running frantically through Union Square and dropping off boxes for the wheatgrass. I remember obsessively checking the rain clouds that were hovering over the park. I remember snapping at my poor mother. I remember being mildly obsessed with the way the unforgiving fabric of my dress was wrinkling across my stomach. I remember worrying about my sister getting out of the twisted Spanx pretzel she'd gotten herself into because I was rushing her. I remember the anxiety over the timing and the music and whether or not my grandmother was going to do something embarrassing in the middle of it all. I worried about tripping on the hem of my dress. I was nervous about the candles, the center-pieces, and the seating chart.

In my haste to remember everything, I forgot to finish writing out two place cards. One of them read simply *Mr. S*, like a 007 character.

It still haunts me.

My father was still alive then. Four days before the big day, he was in the midst of a ragged anxiety breakdown—a fact everyone hid from me to save me the stress. Note: never do that. No one was sure if he was actually going to make it to the cere-mony until about forty-eight hours before. But he did and made a wonderful, touching toast. He danced with me to Louis Armstrong, and one of my favorite photos is a casual snapshot of me sitting in front of my parents, bent like a little girl telling them a story, my hands caught between both of my father's.

After the promises and the cupcakes, our guests piled out in the damp night. My father-in-law, standing up through the open sunroof of a hired limo, pointed guests north, like a slightly tipsy cavalry leader. My grandmother complained about something, because that's what she always did. The catering staff gave us the last bottle of wine in the venue, not so secretly pleased that our wedding party had drunk the bar dry.

Not me. I don't think I had a full glass of wine the entire evening. Somehow, in between the congratulations and the hugs, my glass kept getting whisked away before I could drink it.

And then it was over.

We "I do'ed" and then we were over the threshold, and we were done.

And here we are, two and a half decades later. I'm still apologizing to my mother for being bitchy.

Sorry, Mom.

But all of that? That's a wedding story, not a marriage story.

A QUARTER CENTURY is a long time. It feels like a long time. We're out of the realm of *"Oh, honey, it feels like just yesterday."* Nope. It feels like twenty-five years ago.

In the best possible way, of course.

Twenty-five years is a little more than 9,100 days. Twenty-five years is almost 220,000 hours. Twenty-five years is way too many minutes to sing in a song a la "Seasons of Love."

Twenty-five years have taught me that marriage is not about a specific day or a specific hour. It's not a New York City evening twenty-five years ago or any of the anniversaries marking that day since. It's all the days in between that make up a marriage. And all the days to come.

Saying *"I do"* is the easy part. To keep doing the doing? That's a different story.

That's a marriage story.

WHEN LOVE COMES KNOCK, knock, knocking on your door, it's easy to get caught up in the swoon and swirl of it, in a sticky web of romance novels and glossy magazine spreads. To lose yourself in bold words like forever and soulmate.

It's easy to forget that love is not static. Marriage is not static.

Both are living things, demanding light and water and care, like those green walls that were all the rage at the mall a few years ago. Hearts are tender things and easily bruised, and there are a lot of people who seem to revel in the bruising.

A marriage needs to be fed and looked after. It needs to be brought in from the cold and wrapped in blankets and made a cup of hot tea every now and then. A marriage needs pampering and pruning. It needs alone time and together time, and enough time to take root.

And then, when the roots have set, it needs room to expand.

When you take off the dress with the unforgiving fabric, when you hang up the morning suit, you've got to be willing to get your hands dirty. Put on the stuff you don't mind getting stained and torn to trim back the dead bits. Lash it to a trellis until it gets the hang of growing toward the sun.

Even still, it's inevitable that a thorn will catch you in a soft bit of flesh, startling you with the pain of something so small. Sometimes, a hornet will come out of nowhere and sting you in the ass, taking you by surprise. Both hurt in different ways.

A marriage story is the story of doing it all anyway, getting your hands muddy even when you have a dinner party to go to later. If you're smart, you'll figure out how to use all the bullshit to fertilize the soil so that the pretty things bloom. If you're even smarter, you'll realize sometimes the prettiest blossoms take a few seasons to mature.

That's something that no officiant tells you as you're standing there in a dress or a suit, a pair of jeans, or shorts and flip-flops. That linking your days and nights to someone else is often hard, boring work.

Marriage, like gardening, requires manual labor.

It's not just the wedding days and the party days or the gooey love story that led up to saying yes to the dress; it's about all the days afterward. The fun days and the angry days and all the boring filler days that make up the years.

It took me a while to realize that it's not the angry days you've got to watch out for. The angry days are just that. He left the mug on the counter again. She lied about the dress that she said she didn't buy, but did. Angry days are like a storm; they're loud and scary and sometimes flashy—but often they clear the air and leave you a bit more breathing room.

No, it's not the angry days that are the most dangerous. It's the filler days—because if you're not paying attention, all of a sudden you're forty or fifty or sixty, and the marriage is there, but it's brown and brittle and halfway to dead. Maybe you got caught up in all the other detritus of life and didn't do the weeding. Maybe you didn't cover it before the first frost of the year. Or maybe you thought the other person was doing the maintenance, so it meant you didn't have to. And maybe they were, and then they stopped...*because* they were the only one doing the work. Or maybe you thought that the act of saying "I do" in front of all those dearly beloveds was enough, and by the time you frantically reached for the pruning shears, the whole thing was just a big mass of thorns that was too tangled to hack your way through.

It's not enough just to *be* married. To be married is too passive. You can't just be married. Marriage is active. It's a life of its own with 175,000 moving parts.

You need to **do** marriage.

Not just "I do," but forever "do."

THAT FRIDAY AFTERNOON, the rain held off just long enough, and despite my efforts, the front of my dress wrinkled anyway. There are so many things I would have done differently if I could go back in time. I would definitely have been nicer to my mother, and I would certainly have let my sister dry off completely before trying to squeeze into Spanx. I would have paid more attention to my father and danced with him again. I would have twirled more and talked less. I would have kept a tighter hold on my wine glass.

I would have finished those damn place cards. Mr. S, indeed. I still don't know his last name.

Some things I'd definitely keep, though. The wheatgrass was pretty, and the cupcakes were delicious. The New York City skyline twinkled like fairy lights, as if just for us. The friends, the family.

Oh! And the prince of a man, too.

That's worked out pretty well.

THINGS I ASK MY HUSBAND...

Why does my knee hurt?
Why am I so tired all the time?
Is a carbon monoxide leak making us so tired??
Did I do something to my knee?
Why did I come in here?
How was 1990 35 years ago?
Did you call your mother?
Did I forget I did something to my knee?
Why can't I poop?
Has my neck always looked like this?
Do you really need to eat dinner?
Every night???
Is 9 o'clock too early to go to bed?
Is the wine making me tired?
Is there more wine?
How does the TV work again?
Did I take my pill?

to the girls who shared their aqua net with me

. . .

Whenever I'm visiting the town where I grew up, I get together with a small group of friends from high school. Over the years I've been away, we've expanded and contracted, adding a friend here or there like a charm on a bracelet, but at its center is a core group of four. And although it's been nearly forty years since we threw our mortarboards into a cloudy June sky, it's the easiest thing in the world to slip back into a friendship that is comfortable and uncomplicated.

Light as a feather, stiff as a board. It was a girlhood game we played at slumber parties, but it's an apt description of our friendship, too. The responsibility for maintaining the bond doesn't weigh heavy upon me, but I know, without having to think about it too much, that it would bear whatever weight I put on it. The four of us have a shared past of acne and baby fat, of questionable fashion choices, crushes, and teenage heartbreak. The foundation of our relationship was forged in the intensity of adolescence; it holds the giggles and the tears, questions whispered in the dark, and tips on how to use a tampon.

You can't fake that stuff. It's the base that I built myself on.

There's no need to impress them. When we meet at my mother's house, I throw some chips in a bowl, open a tub of ready-made dip, and make sure I have enough wine. That's about it. These women have seen me at my gawkiest, my gothiest, my geekiest. These are the girls who snuck wine coolers at the bridge with me, who gave me endless rides and refuge, who slept out for Duran Duran tickets and screamed themselves hoarse alongside me when Simon le Bon sang about "da Reflex." They are the girls who shared their Aqua Net with me, who let me primp in the magnetic mirror on the inside of their locker, and who stood in a circle and danced to "We're Not Gonna Take It."

Once you've white-girl danced to Twisted Sister in a sweaty cafeteria together, it's hard to impress someone.

Sometimes, when we're together, it's hard to get *past* the past. In my head—and often aloud—I still refer to them by their maiden names. It's difficult sometimes to think of Kelly as a veterinarian instead of Kelly, who adored Howard Jones, rocked a crimp, and lived around the block. It's hard to think of Joanne as the mother of two adult women, now a grandmother, and not Joanne, whose house we always hung out at, who drove us everywhere, who once came to the door to collect me after an argument with my mother. It's hard to think of Diane as anything but the perky cheerleader who was hiding her physical pain behind her smile, who used to make me sit in cold hockey rinks to watch her boyfriend play, and who always made me promise to ring once when I got home.

She still does that, actually, even though we're in our fifties.

Our paths have converged and diverged at various forks. I've moved abroad, and Diane lives in the same town we grew up in. Joanne had her kids young; I had them late. Kelly married her high school crush, who was my date to one of those dances in the gym where we wore taffeta monstrosities. But we have this core, this commonality that draws us like moths to a flame, a history of having survived the same hallways and the same classrooms, of growing up and surviving adolescence relatively intact.

We still talk about boys—though now it's not who we're sweet on, but our husbands and sons. We talk about the parents that some of us still have, and we reminisce about the ones who are not there anymore.

"Remember how your dad used to answer the phone?" Diane always says. And we laugh because my father was a class A pain in the ass.

We still gossip about who did what to who in high school. Over the years, a few long-held secrets have been shared over the rosé and spinach dip.

We trade memories like baseball cards. We tell stories because that's how women connect, through our stories. Sometimes we remember things differently, or in my case, not at all. We were so caught up in our own heads, so focused on the girl in the mirror gazing back, that we often didn't see past the cloud of hairspray to the girl standing to the right or left. Whenever I'm caught in a memory black hole, I reach out to Diane, who seems to have total recall. Joanne keeps the proof of cringy hairstyles and botched fashion choices in boxes of photographs. Kelly remembers names and people that I do not.

We're far enough past it all now to laugh. Mostly.

In all these years, the conversations haven't changed too much, but *we* have changed.

Diane has two new hips, her old ones worn down by juvenile arthritis. Kelly's hair is no longer crimped, though it's still thick. Joanne—annoyingly—looks the same as she did in high school. I am softer around the edges. And the middle, top, bottom, and sides. We all have to pull out our glasses to read the menu when we go out and use the flashlight on our phones, like grannies in training.

Despite the softening of jawlines, despite the need for

reading glasses, we're in agreement that we all look better than we did in high school. Not just because we use less hairspray and make better fashion choices, not due to filling out or even tightening up, but because on the other side of the girlhood door, we found the women we were meant to be.

These girls! These women! They witnessed my transformation from tall, geeky girl to a tall eyeliner goth. With them, I am not Dina, the writer, or Dina, who lives abroad; I am the gawky girl who had a crush on the quarterback. I am the girl who didn't get asked to the prom, the one who, even at sixteen, was railing about the injustices of high school life in the school newspaper. Someday, I'll get Diane to tell you about the Bus Barn incident. I am the caterpillar who built a cocoon around myself to survive, who didn't blossom into a butterfly until well after high school.

These women know from whence I came. They keep me honest. They ground me; I can't pretend to be anything other than who I am around them.

Whenever I'm feeling lost or unsure, knowing they are there is a safe space of sorts. When I think I've changed, they remind me that I haven't, not all that much. That the bones of who I am have always been there. Through their eyes, I can see that the girl I was is still present in the woman I am—without having to reach for my glasses.

Often, the past can feel more like handcuffs, binds that keep you from changing. But these friendships, born of blue eyeshadow and sky-high hair, of concert tickets and cafeteria dances, of sitting on a concrete curb by the bridge and whispering dreams to a night sky of shooting stars—they feel like home.

Thank you for being there then and for being there now, even when the miles and the months stretch between us. Thank you for reminding me that the awkward girl from grade school and the punkish one from high school are still there, along with the woman who swears too much and writes words about it all.

Most of all, thank you for loving all of them.

mulberry court

. . .

By the time this goes to print, my in-laws will have moved from the house they called home for almost fifty years. Things will have started to settle, like a bad perm or dust on the mantelpiece tchotchkes that survived the downsizing cull.

Any move drags a maelstrom of feelings in its wake. When it's a family home, one lived in for decades, the feelings are bigger and bolder, ripe with things that have been hidden or forgotten. Tell-tale heartbreaks under the floorboards and laughter caught in the eaves.

Most of the memories of the house on Mulberry Court aren't mine. The trees don't hold my secrets; the fireflies caught in the grass belonged to someone else. As does the hamster I'm fairly sure is still buried somewhere in the garden.

Still, there are enough of my own recollections strewn throughout, draped over the furniture like a blanket. I've spent nearly twenty-eight years sleeping in the spare room upstairs, drinking coffee in the kitchen, and having dinners and holidays around the dining room table with wedding crystal and heirloom cheese knives.

That dining room is where I met my husband's entire family for the first time, it's where I learned to use chopsticks, and it's where I heard the stories about the boy who grew into the man I fell in love with.

When our children were young, we spent every other Christmas there, dragging babies and presents on planes, trains, and automobiles. On Christmas morning, they dug through heavy stockings in front of the fireplace. They fed the ducks at the pond down the road and spun themselves nauseous on the merry-go-round at the grassy common. We've been on a hundred muddy walks through the local woods and sat in the sunshine on pub picnic tables more times than I can count.

Over the years, I've gone from guest to daughter-in-law, from being served dinner to peeling potatoes on the kitchen island and making cups of tea in delicate porcelain mugs that I take to the garden, head tilted toward the fickle English sun.

Mulberry Court is not mine, but it holds a lot of me.

THE LAST TIME I was at the house, the decision to move didn't seem to have any real weight behind it. Sleeping in the room we always sleep in, sipping coffee at the same kitchen island, eating around the same table, it never occurred to me that the visit would be my last.

"Do you want the dressing gown?" My husband asked me when his parents told us they'd made the decision to move.

For nearly twenty-eight years, my mother-in-law has left a dressing gown on the back of the guest room door for me. A small act of terry-cloth kindness. And for twenty-eight years, I've used it, always returning it to the back of the bedroom door, where it hangs in the vague shape of me.

"I think it's served its purpose," I said. "We can retire it with full honors."

There will be boxes to pack up, a lifetime divided into piles.

Take, sell, donate. It's a difficult thing to divide a life like that—I speak from experience. Of course, we haven't lived in any one place nearly as long—when the collectibles have collectibles and drawers are filled with expired medication and receipts from appliances that stopped working long ago.

The clearing, the decluttering, the choosing what to keep and what to chuck—it's exhausting. Whenever I visit my own mother, I try to get a head start on the process. With the same faux enthusiasm I used to use to persuade my children to *just try the broccoli*, I try to persuade her to think about downsizing her extensive collection of throw pillows.

"You know that Karen and I are going to have to do this after you die, right?" I tease her, but almost immediately, I feel terrible about it.

It's never *really* about the reluctance to part with the throw pillows or the decorative plates or even the heirloom cheese knives; it's about the passage of time, of trying to make sense of where it's all gone, and just how much of it is left.

I TRY NOT to think of home as a physical place, a space with a roof and floor and indoor plumbing. Because we've moved around, for us, home isn't bound to geography, to street names and postal codes, as much as where we are all together. Our kids have never had the security blanket of a childhood home in the way that I do, or my husband does.

Or did.

In that way, our childhood homes became an anchor for us all. We relied on the roofs and floors and indoor plumbing of our respective family homes to serve as a sort of HQ, a port in any storm, even if it was only for a few weeks out of the year. We knew we had a place there.

There's something weird and time-loopy about being in your childhood home. Everyone sort of slips into the roles they assumed in childhood, even though we're all well into adulthood and have long outgrown those childhood skins.

When we were fledgling adults, going home was a mini-respite from our own grown-up-ness. Parents were still parents. They still made decisions, cooked food, hosted holidays, and paid for the restaurant tab.

Over time, there was a generation shift, a slow continental drift.

We started hosting the holidays. When we spent time at our respective parents' homes, we took on more of the meal planning and prep. We cleared out basements and garages and gently—or not so gently in my case—encouraged decluttering and downsizing.

When my six-foot-something sons visit my mother's house now, not only do they not fit in the beds with the Star Wars sheets they spent summers sleeping in, but they are seasonal day laborers. I put them to work, hacking down the wilds of the backyard with a mini chainsaw and hauling bags to the dump.

At my in-laws, we slowly transitioned from Granny's Sunday dinners to taking over the cooking or eating out.

Bit by bit, we reduced the burden until we bore the brunt of it.

When the lights are dimmed for the last time and the front door key is handed over, it's more than just another slow tectonic plate movement shift. It's aging parents, aging children, and the aging reflection that stares back at you from the mirror. It's Hannibal crossing the Alps and no going backsies. It's crossing the threshold for good.

"I guess this makes us the anchor now," I said to my husband.

THROUGHOUT ALL OF the preparations and decision-making, I keep checking in with my husband. Though the idea of moving had been hanging around for a while, the final decision felt sudden. It didn't take us aback, but maybe it took us aside.

We've talked about what it all means emotionally and logistically, what it means for the future. It will change the way we visit, for how long, and at what times of year. That stuff is the easy stuff in a way, answered with hotel reservations and creative planning.

It's the other stuff that catches you by surprise, like a half-buried root that snags the tip of your sneaker and sends you flying across the grass.

The things are things; even the most fragile among them can be wrapped in a cotton candy cloud of bubble wrap and transported from one place to the next.

The memories and feelings that are unearthed are trickier, ghosts that rise when you pull up a carpet or handwritten notes that have fallen behind the hutch.

Look, remember? That's where I skinned my knee when I fell off my skateboard that summer! Do you remember that day, the one when we rode our bikes all the way to the next town over, and we found that stream that was singing with toads? Do you remember the birthdays we had in the back garden, or the time I got locked out, or how we used to roll a ball from bedroom to bedroom at night before Dad would stomp up the stairs full of bluster?

The house on Mulberry Court holds the ghost of my husband's childhood, long before he met me. Whenever I was there, it was like a guided tour through his past, the photos scattered on the bookcases and the stories told around the dining table. I've heard the stories of family vacations so many times, I feel like I was there, a ghost of the future, sitting on his shoulder.

Don't go swimming; you're going to get swimmer's ear! I want to shout at him. Don't kiss that girl in Sardinia; you're going to end up with mono! Don't cry too hard over the Dreaded Polly; it will all work out, I promise.

All those building blocks of the man I met, yet to be put together. The genesis is hidden there, in the wall-to-wall carpeting and the tiny bedroom where he used to fold his too-tall self into a too-small bed. It's been a long time since he's walked into the front door with frequency. He lived there for less time than we've been together, and yet, the house will always be home for him, not only where he grew up but also where he grew into who he is.

Saying goodbye to the house is saying goodbye to the walls that bore witness to all of those things. It's up to us to keep them alive.

In the stories that we tell our children, and perhaps one day they'll tell their children, there will be a version of the house on Mulberry Court. It will live on in memories and recollections, in photographs and stories.

The very things that will anchor us, no matter where we're docked.

crush

. . .

My first real heart-flutter crush was on Craig of the Blond Hair. Blue-eyed Craig, in his Pop Warner football jacket, strutting around like a fourth-grade peacock. A little bit Ricky Schroder, a little bit Bo Duke, hair the color of a Midwestern summer sun.

I fell hard.

I'm not sure what happened to Craig, whether he moved towns or switched schools, but the shape of him lives rent-free in my childhood memories. The next time I see Diane, I'll ask her; she'll remember, I'm sure.

No matter, there were plenty of others to take his place. They appeared and disappeared in a parade of quasi-swooniness. Crushes that lasted a day or a month or all through high school. My heart would flutter when they walked by—pitter pat, pitter pat. Pressed against the cool wall of the high school cafeteria, I breathlessly waited for them to assume the leading man role in my crush fantasy, to help me enact the perfect movie ending. Richard Gere swooping me up in his arms. Jake Ryan waiting in his red Porsche after the wedding. What about prom, Blaine?

The happily ever after rarely happened, though there were a

few slow dances to Whitney Houston and some basement make-out sessions. There were bad boys and quiet boys and an alarming number of boys who wanted to go through me to get to my best friend.

Such is the beauty of the crush. It's not as all-consuming as first love, nor as devastating as a heartbreak. It's a frothy, daydreamy, spin-the-bottle fantasy. A heady secret you carry around in your pocket or ink onto diary pages with pens that smell like raspberries.

Dear Diary,
Craig of the Blond Hair smiled at me during math class! He is sooooo cute. At lunch, Chrissy told me she heard he's going to ask AnnMarie to the dance, and ugghhhh, why???? I might die!!!!

In high school, I had such an intense crush on Simon Le Bon that when the boat he was sailing on capsized, I was glued to the news like a captain's wife, waiting for word from her seafaring beloved. Later, forced to choose a confirmation name, I asked for Simon.

They refused.

In college, I had a crush on my Intro to Women's Studies professor. It wasn't a sexual crush; I just wanted to be around her. I didn't fantasize about kissing her; I wanted to be her, or at least near enough that her passion and intelligence rubbed off on me.

I've had crushes on bartenders and colleagues, strangers, musicians, and movie stars. Once I'd been out in the real world and met my fair share of Craigs and Jakes and perennially disappointing Blaines, the crush took a more nuanced turn. They were less about a person as a whole and more about some thing or things that I found deeply attractive.

I had a crush on a movie star's forearms once. And on another one's hair. I've had crushes on characters from both books and films. I'll swoon for you forever, Colonel Brandon.

Still? Always.

My crush on Alan Rickman continues into his afterlife.

DESPITE MY EXTENSIVE EXPERIENCE, middle age has thrown a new one at me that I wasn't expecting: the *Mom Crush*. The Mom Crush is not a crush on other mothers, though I've had those too; no, the Mom Crush is that cookie-dough, apron-ish squishy feeling you get when you meet a teen or young adult that you want to do motherly things for.

The Mom Crush is not about taking someone *to* bed. It's about wanting to tuck them *into* bed with a glass of warm milk and making sure they have clean socks.

Metaphorically, of course. I'm not a creep.

Here's an example.

Marcus Rashford is an English footballer who plays for the team my husband supports. I don't watch football, but since it seems to be on twenty-four seven in my home, I absorb a lot *about* football, even if it's just over my laptop. Years ago, my husband watched a television program about Rashford that detailed his early life and how he'd been raised by a single mom who instilled in him a sense of humility that came across the screen.

I listened. Then I closed my laptop and watched and... I was smitten. Not with this young man, who was literally young enough to be my son, *but by his story.*

Since then, I've had a totally irrational interest in Marcus Rashford's career. I'm invested in his success. I want him to do well, and when he does, I feel an odd sense of pride that feels like it emanates from some communal well of motherhood. I root for him, I smile when my husband or sons tell me that he's scored, and I am offended on his behalf when he's not chosen to play.

There was something about his story that made my Bat Mom ears perk up, which, in turn, triggered an aura of maternal protectiveness that I beamed in his general direction.

I told you. It's weird.

LIKE CHEESE, wine, and Idris Elba, the middle-aged crush has mellowed and softened into something different than those early, heady crushes of yore. It's sometimes a bit awkward explaining that when I, a fifty-something mom of two, say *he's adorable,* I don't mean he's hot, fit, rizzled up, or whatever the hunky word du jour is.

I mean that if said young man showed up and I had just baked a batch of brownies, I would give him one while it was still warm.

I'm not using "warm baked goods" as a euphemism; I'm being literal. If Leo Woodall showed up at my door, I would invite him in and give him a square of cooked batter, like Mrs. Cunningham fussing over the Fonz.

I do wonder if there is an equivalent Dad crush, one that is less Lester Burnham in *American Beauty and* more Mr. Rogers. Then again, if a gray-haired man in a cardigan asked a young girl, *"Won't you be my neighbor?"* who could blame her if she ran in the opposite direction?

I like to think there are dads who happened to watch a show about the rise of women's football and now find themselves not lusting after the sporty ladies but simply beaming good dad thoughts into the universe, rooting for them to get paid what they deserve.

. . .

A FEW MONTHS after Captain Le Bon's boat capsized and he was safely returned to land, he got married, breaking my fifteen-year-old heart as only a celebrity crush can. It seems a long time ago I was forced to accept that he was not going to spot me in a crowded arena, overlook the eleven-year age gap, and whisk me off my feet and carry me toward the movie ending.

It's been even longer since I waited in a sweaty cafeteria, hoping the crush would ask me to dance to "Purple Rain," and longer again since Craig of the Blond Hair first set my little fourth-grade heart aflutter with his grade-school swagger.

In the end, I did get a version of happily ever after, tailored just for me. His entrance on the scene was a decade too late to take me to prom, but he's taken me to a few weddings over the years, including our own. At this stage, asking him to swoop me off my feet would likely result in permanent injury.

Sometimes, even all these years later, I'll catch a glimpse of him across a room, telling a story to someone else, and my heart beats a little faster.

Still? Always.

DEAR DIARY,

THERE WAS THIS REALLY HOT GUY AT THE PARTY TONIGHT. TALL, DARK, AND HANDSOME. I'M SO LUCKY I GET TO TAKE HIM HOME. I THINK I'M GOING TO ASK SIRI TO PLAY PURPLE RAIN AND SEE IF HE'LL DANCE WITH ME...

♥ ♥
♥

left to my own devices, or the one where i reach full old lady potential

. . .

My father was home every night at five o'clock, his mechanic hands sometimes still bearing the grease of the day when he sat at the kitchen table. The four of us sat, chewing meatloaf or spooning mashed potatoes into our mouths. If the phone rang while we were still eating, he'd reach behind to where it hung on the kitchen wall, pick it up, and say, "*We're having supper; call back later.*"

Then he'd hang up.

When there were house phones with cords that only stretched so far, everyone knew the rules. When long-distance plans were so expensive that you waited until after nine pm to call, but only for five minutes, everyone understood the rules.

You didn't call during supper, and you definitely didn't call late at night unless it was an emergency, because the lone phone on the kitchen wall would wake the entire house, and maybe the neighbor if they were close enough.

Contrary to what I thought in sixth grade, coordinating my outfit with my best friend was not considered an emergency.

We're having supper. Call back later.

. . .

In my own little family of four, I am the least technologically literate. While the rest of them do almost everything on their phones, I cling to my laptop like it's a buoyant life preserver keeping me afloat in a sea of gadgets and whizzdings. For one, I can actually *see* the screen without having to continually increase the font. Also, most of my days are spent clacking away on a keyboard. Just thinking about trying to do that on a phone makes me break out in stress hives.

But there is also this: I don't like my phone that much.

I don't use my phone to pay for or order things. I've only recently started using it for boarding passes, and I still like to have a printed one in my bag because I don't trust my phone. While I do keep a family calendar on my phone, I also have a desk diary that I use as my primary source for keeping track of where I need to be. I use my phone for photos, but when we go on vacation, I still take my trusty point-and-click.

For the most part, I use my phone the way I used to use the kitchen phone when I was growing up. I'm not lying on the floor with my feet up on the door jamb, talking to my best friend, but I still mostly use my phone to communicate. There is less talking and more WhatsApping, but the underlying idea is the same as it was all those years ago when I was trying to figure out if the quarterback liked me back: an exchange of information.

I wouldn't call myself anti-technology, but I'm not **anti**-anti-technology either; I'm sort of a tech agnostic. Increasingly, I feel like, in terms of everyday usefulness, I've peaked. I have summited the mountain of convenience, and here I stand at the top, my flimsy white flag whipping in the wind.

Instead of continuing to make my life simpler and easier, more often than not, it feels like I'm going in the other direction.

Are there apps, programs, and parts of technology that make my life easier and more convenient? Absolutely. Not having to write checks features heavily on my list of pros. Setting up appointments online, especially when you live in a place where you're not fluent in the language, is a lifesaver. Google Translate, travel bookings, restaurant reservations, and other techy bells and whistles that allow me to avoid face-to-face communication and telephone calls? All used and appreciated.

I'm not denying there are great things about technology—lots of them—but as a card-carrying member of Gen X, who had one foot in analog and the other in digital, who came of age with a handful of television channels only to spend the second half of my life unable to work my television, I feel I'm qualified to say that *life wasn't all that hard before.*

It just wasn't. The hard bits about life, the heartbreaks and job losses, the uncertainty, the sicknesses and struggles, and global catastrophes are *still* hard—technology hasn't made life's difficulties go away.

There is still no Rosie Jetson robo-whisking dinner for me.

Is the quality of my life vastly improved by being able to ask Siri to set a timer rather than setting one in the shape of a boiled egg? Not really. Is the ability to track my family wherever they are in the world, like a live-action Carmen San Diego, helpful? The jury is out on that one. I know people who, if they can't see exactly where their children are at all times, freak out that those same children have been chopped into Hansel and Gretel pieces in a dark wood.

Hi, it's me. I'm people.

My parents simply assumed I was fine unless they heard differently—and no one was calling past 9 pm. They slept soundly.

We're sleeping; call back later.

I AM A TYPE A VIRGO, First Born, Oldest Sister model 1.0. Efficiency is my kink. My husband provides me with evidence of his efficiency as a form of foreplay. Yet all the stuff that is *supposed* to make my life more efficient often just makes it more complicated. It's a lot of flashing lights and haptic noises, and I'm no longer sure that what I get in return is worth all the updating.

More and more, I find myself longing for the straightforwardness of those analog days of yore, when video games meant Asteroids at Skate Palace and viral meant a stomach flu that kept you home with the plastic puke bowl, the same one we all used for popcorn.

As much as writing checks was a bore of a chore, it wasn't hard. Now paying a bill sometimes involves two devices, one that uses a thumbprint and one to receive a one-time code, verifications, authenticators, and face recognition. And a pin for good measure.

Sometimes, I think the checks were easier.

In my childhood home, when supper was over, the meatloaf masticated, and the green beans gobbled, my sister and I would take turns in the bath, and then we'd all sit in the family room to watch television. We had our places—mine was on the carpet with my back to the wood stove, or sometimes in front of the hot air vent with a blanket. I was a cold child. Someone would get up and turn the television on, and on that channel it would stay until someone else got up to change it.

Mork & Mindy or *The Muppet Show. Donny and Marie, Laverne & Shirley*. There were Tuesday night lineups and Sunday night family hours. You ran to the bathroom during the commercial breaks and hoped you made it back in time. Every November around Thanksgiving, my sister and I waited for *The Sound of Music* to air. Christmas specials were on for two weeks in December. And once a year, we sang Supercalifragilisticexpialidocious along with Mary Poppins.

It all seems so quaint now, like we were channeling Laura Ingalls Wilder on the frontier.

I DON'T KNOW how to use our current television. There are VPNs, HDMI choices, and passwords to the fifty-two streaming services. There is more than one remote. There's a cable box and an Apple TV box and a virtual Sky box, and somehow, I think, these are all connected to the router, which I have the password to somewhere, though I'm not one hundred percent sure where.

Television is no longer a family activity. There is no Tuesday lineup or Sunday family hour. On demand means no one is waiting until November to sing about whiskers on kittens and warm woolen mittens. We're in different rooms arguing about who is using the Netflix password. When we watch things, it's often alone, under a pair of headphones. On several occasions, I've made a recommendation to one of my sons only to have them tell me they've already seen it, and I'm left trying to figure out how and when they watched ten seasons of *Friends*, eight seasons of *Brooklyn Nine-Nine*, and however many seasons there are of *The Boys* without me even being aware.

The family movie nights we had when they were younger feel like a throwback, not quite as far back as Laura Ingalls Wilder, but maybe the sock hop happy days of the 50s.

It was exciting not to have to get up to manually change the channel when remote controls became standard. TiVo was a revelation, and the pause button? Well, that definitely made using the bathroom a much less frantic endeavor.

But honestly? It wasn't that bad before.

We're watching *Happy Days*; call back later.

SOMETIMES PEOPLE ASK, a bit incredulously, "But would you go back, back to the before times?" as if the before times were so bad, like we were all out foraging for berries and yams, whittling by the fire.

You were there, fellow Xers.

Was it so terrible waiting until September to catch a new season of *The A-Team*? Was it the worst thing in the world to thumb through an encyclopedia for a report on the nervous system, to wait until after dinner to make a phone call, or to spend a day reading a book under a tree when your friends were visiting far-away grandparents?

Have we all forgotten what it's like to ring a doorbell to see if Janie was home?

God, here I am doing that thing I always said I would never do.
Should I say it?
Yes, I'm going to say it.
In a lot of ways, things weren't just easier; they were better.

LIKE MANY FAMILIES, we have a rule about *no phones at the dinner table*—or it was a rule when the children were shorter than me. Now it's more of a request that I struggle to get everyone to honor. In a win for women's clothing, my pockets aren't big enough for my phone, which means it's never with me when we're sitting down to eat. My males? Their phones are in their pockets at all times, radiating God knows what onto their important bits, but what do I know? I'm just a mom.

Their phones are *always* there. With them, extensions of themselves.

If someone makes a joke or a reference, if someone has a question or needs to explain something, before I can put the spoon back in the pasta bowl, someone's got their phone out looking it up.

Were we all just more patient twenty or thirty years ago, with our low-tech answering machines and busy signals? Did we simply have lower expectations?

Not that long ago, my husband and I were at a dinner party, and I left my phone in another room. My teenager later told me he was frustrated that he couldn't reach me immediately to ask a question, relay information, or get permission for something.

"I was having dinner," I said. "I called you back later."

We used to be better at waiting. At reasoning. At just leaving questions open-ended without the answer, or making educated guesses. Or just not knowing. There was something peaceful about accepting that there were things simply out of reach.

Things were ok without the immediacy that technology demands of us.

We managed.

We're thinking; call back later.

I'VE STARTED LEAVING my phone at home when I go out. The first time was accidental, and I admit, I freaked out because what if someone needed to reach me? *What if, indeed?* For more than half of my life, I was fine with the idea of not being immediately reachable. I left messages. I figured things out. I asked for directions. When I traveled, I wrote postcards to let everyone know that I was alive and wished they were there.

When I am home now, I leave my phone in another room. This way, I can't hear any of the notification tinkles and tones that alert me to one of a hundred different things I apparently need to be alerted about a thousand times a day. Emails and WhatsApps and texts and six different messenger platforms.

If someone needs to reach me that badly, they'll call.

But not after 9 pm, please, unless it's an emergency.

I'm living; call back later.

interlude

Smile at the phone
College son is calling me!
Oh. He needs money

———————

once upon a menopause

· · ·

I wish I could tell you a story of witchcraft and spells, of maidens and mothers and crones. But I've learned that I'm not so good with fiction. I'm much better at these tales and stories that hold seedlings of truth that bloom into something else.

In any case, this story has most of those things, maybe just not in the way we're used to seeing them.

A (NOT ALL THAT) long time ago, my body began to change, almost in front of my eyes. It wasn't quite as dramatic as transitioning into a werewolf under the light of a full moon...but it wasn't too far off. There were embers of heat that flared and subsided, small stars blinking in my veins. There was a pea soup fog that settled over my brain like a woolen cloak. There was blinding rage over inconsequential things like sticky spaghetti and sorrow so deep that sometimes I couldn't find anything to span the river it ran through me.

Perhaps, in hindsight, the canines, claws, and wolfish howls might have been easier.

What I remember the most about that time is that when anyone asked how I was feeling, my answer was always the same.

How do I feel? *Untethered.*

In flailing around for some sort of meaning, "untethered" was the closest word I could find to describe the sense I had of being unmoored, disconnected from everything: my body, the world around me, and especially myself. I felt unloved and misunderstood. I felt taken for granted and ignored. I felt out of control of my emotions, my moods, and my body. And I, who use words for a living, could not find the right ones to make anyone else understand what was happening. Mostly because I did not understand it myself.

I couldn't escape the claustrophobia of my thoughts or the fire in my blood. I could feel the mists of rage descending, but I couldn't stop them from enveloping me. It felt like heartbreak. It felt like grief. It felt like betrayal.

When I looked at my reflection, I was often stunned at the face staring back at me. Whoever it was *looked* like me, but a bit crazed. A Disney villain, a funhouse harridan.

I was an old movie reel playing to an audience of one, scratchy and jumpy. Every now and then, I would get stuck, and all the struts and structures that had held me together for forty-eight years would pool into a melted, gooey mess at my feet.

It was like I was living in someone else's body, my real self watching from a distance, but close enough that I could still feel the heat coming off her skin in waves.

At the time, I didn't understand the truth in that statement, because it *was* someone else's body. A new version of me was tearing through the bones and skin of the old one. Not like a butterfly gradually emerging from a cocoon, all lovely and gossamer-winged—more like an alien ripping through a thorax.

If that sounds violent, it's because it was.

. . .

UNTIL FAIRLY RECENTLY, no one talked about menopause outside the groups of women you'd spy in kitchen corners or by an open window. Even a few years ago, when I was experiencing most of this, you were essentially dumped at sea and left to sink or swim. In the meantime, your skin starts to itch, and chin hairs sprout like fly legs in the space of a minute. You can't sleep. Things that worked perfectly well yesterday ache the next morning.

I was constantly asking my husband, "Did I do something to my shoulder and just forget? My wrist? The back of my knee? The second knuckle of my third finger on my left hand?"

My hair started to fall out, not in clumps, but in strands that blanketed my bathroom floor and clogged the shower drain. I lost two teeth to infection. Could it be related to peri-menopause? I asked the dentist as she yanked one from my jaw.

"Not sure," she said, tossing my tooth in the bin. "No research."

I cried and sweated, and I raged, raged against the dying of light and the coming of the morn and all the hours in between.

The experience was terrifying and disconcerting and discom-bobulating and lots of other adjectives it would take me too long to write. Yet, somewhere in the midst of all of that, there was a tiny piece of me that understood that eventually, I would be on the other side of it all. She was still too far away to see clearly, but on some witchy level of consciousness, I understood that there was a chrysalis-crone waiting for me on the far shores of the mists of menopause.

I just had to get there.

I held on to that scrap of knowledge like a lifeline. I wore it around my neck like an amulet, a vial of my own essence and some eye of newt for good measure.

. . .

Now, I can put the pieces in an order that makes sense, but in the thick of it, it was like trying to finish a jigsaw puzzle without an image, just a massive pile of blank cardboard pieces.

I was in my late 30s when I started to experience what I can now clearly recognize as perimenopause symptoms. I'm not sure I'd heard the term before, but more, it never even occurred to me to have my hormone levels tested. I was still chasing a toddler around, and menopause seemed far in the future. Instead, I chalked the increasing episodes of rage, the heart palpitations, and the agitation up to other things. Postpartum depression, life changes, and general aging. We had undertaken a massive overseas move, leaving our lives behind for something that looked completely different. Surely that was it, I told myself again and again. And it probably *was* all of those things, but no doubt all of those things were exacerbated by the fact that my hormones were planning their retirement party.

I was under 40. Menopause was the stuff of old ladies in sensible shoes, not thirty-eight-year-old moms.

Determined to regain control, I started with what I felt was most within my control: my weight. With pregnancies firmly in the rearview mirror and forty around the next curve, I set out to shed the last of the baby weight. In reality, I starved and hill-walked myself down to nothing. Take that, Mother Nature. Who's in control now, bitch?

But as more birthdays in my fifth decade came and went, I was steadily gaining weight that would not budge. Or it would budge for a few months, then come back with friends. All my usual tricks failed. I counted calories, I walked, I biked everywhere, and for a while it worked. Until it didn't.

Eventually, I gave up trying. I bought looser clothes and avoided the scale. But after one summer of super-sized gluttony in the US, even I knew I had reached a point where something was going to have to give, and not just because even my elasticated pants were getting tight. If I had been uncomfortable before, then I was downright miserable. The weight I was carrying was in fun new places. My limbs looked different. My knees started to ache.

I felt like I was wearing someone else's body on top of my own.

When I did eventually step on the scale, I almost laughed. I was exactly the same weight I'd been at the end of both of my pregnancies.

When I was carrying my sons, I reasoned that my body needed the extra pounds to get through the physical toll of growing a life. But standing there alone in my bathroom, I was definitely not pregnant—in fact, I was as non-pregnant as one could be—yet my body was doing the same thing—squirreling away fat. At least with my pregnancies, there was something tangible to bring home at the end of them, a new something, a beginning.

It took far too long to make the connection between weight gain, birth, and new beginnings. Because what was I doing if not birthing a brand-new version of myself?

Apparently, my body just needed to stuff itself with Pringles and rosé to get the job done.

IT TAKES time to adjust to any new version of yourself. The adult self that emerges after puberty. The softer self that often appears after childbirth. We're quick to tell new mothers to take it easy and to look after themselves, to be kind to themselves. And for good reason.

No one advised me to be gentle with myself while I fumbled about, trying to get used to this new version of myself. No one reminded me that my body had just gone through a massive physical and psychological upheaval.

We tend to think of menopause as one big change that affects our reproductive system, but that's totally wrong. It's not a single change; it's a years-long series of adjustments, transitions, developments, and transformations. It's a total system overhaul. It affects your brain and your bones as well as your emotions and your hormones. It affects your blood cholesterol and your organ functions, your skin and hair, moods and anxieties.

Once I was able to recognize that, once I started treating myself like a new mother of a new me, I started to take better care of myself.

When you are deep in the dense forest of change—puberty, pregnancy, or menopause—it's hard to see anything other than what is directly in front of you. When you're pregnant and you have to pee every minute, it's hard to focus on anything but finding the nearest toilet. When you're in the middle of a hot flash, trying to dab at the sweat snaking a trail through your foundation, all you can think about is getting to the nearest window.

It's hard to see two feet in front of your nose, let alone two years down the road.

Eventually, I got close enough that I could put my hand through the fog and see my fingers wiggling on the other side. The blinding rage subsided—somewhat—until I was angry at the things I *should* be angry at. The hot flashes ebbed to something warm, bits of charcoal that still flare orange every now and then. I surfaced from the depths of the deep, deep sorrow and swam to a new, unexplored shore.

Slowly, hand over hand, I pulled myself downward and re-tethered myself. I put down roots in the newly tilled soil of me.

Some time later, walking through April snowflakes in a city that's not quite mine, I had a moment of blinding clarity. One of those sun-comes-out-from-behind-the-clouds moments. I am well and truly on the other side of all of this change now—the return policy lapsed, and I have no choice but to keep the woman I am.

It's true that menopause is a bitch, but she's a bitch with a plan *and* a gift. She is working hard to craft a version of you that is righteous and true, whose fingertips crackle with electric wisdom. If you haven't met her yet, you're going to love her when you do, even if she has hair on her chin and snarls a bit.

In fact, maybe because of that.

And if you're the one sleeping next to this amazing new being? Be gentle.

She's just given birth to herself.

ONCE UPON A TIME, there was a maiden. She met a prince and had two little princelings who grew and grew like the trees in the forest around her. Some time later, after they had all lived in the forest for a long time, the mother felt a warm buzzing in her blood. She started to eat all the berries in the forest and even some of the bark. Sometimes she howled at the prince, the princelings, and even the moon. The mother was sure that she had done something wrong and that, as punishment, Mother Nature had cast a terrible spell upon her.

What had she done to bring such a curse down upon herself? She yelled at the clouds and the trees, looking for answers. She would often wander alone until she came to the banks of the river called Sorrow, where she would sit alone and weep.

One day, as she was standing to leave, the mother gazed into the river's water, expecting to see her reflection. Instead, staring back at her was someone she did not recognize. Who is that woman, the mother wondered, with her wild hair and her fierce expression? The mother reached down to touch the face staring back at her and watched as the water rippled outward. When it finally settled, the mother could see that she had been wrong; the reflection was her, just a newer version of herself. And just like that, the spell that wasn't really a spell was lifted.

The crone understood that Mother Nature hadn't been angry with her at all but had been leading her to this moment, when her true self would be revealed.

And the crone, once a mother and before that a maiden, went off to live happily ever after and scare small children with her chin hair.

The End.

See? Told you I was better with nonfiction.

the day i turned
into my nana

. . .

It was the foil,
I think—
when I caught myself
smoothing aluminum sheets,
facets catching in the sun,
salvaging tin
for another day

or maybe
it was the plastic bags.

My grandmother had sandwich bags
rinsed clean, draped & drip
drying over the cold water tap
I haven't done that yet,
the Ziploc launder
though it seems wasteful not to, if you think about it.

My Nana also carried
folded tissues in her pocketbook for

wiping public toilet seats & wiping
other seats & I think that's a pretty good idea
actually,

it's only a matter of time
before there are tissues in my pocketbook
or tucked in a cardigan sleeve.

When she died
we went through the remnants of a life
and found a lifetime supply of foil
not delicately refolded,
salvaged for a picnic day
or an impromptu sandwich to be eaten en plein air
but reams and rolls of it
unused
pristine and shiny
stored in sentinel stacks
enough for an advancing army
or a conspiracy convention—

No one knew why
she had so much
& yet still saved scraps like a crow
almost as if she wouldn't use
the shiny stuff
for herself.

Make sure you save the foil from your sandwich
I say to my son each morning
while I organize a drawer of
plastic bags to reuse on
tomorrows & aftermorrows
& every day the foil comes back a wadded tin ball

amongst the crumbs

It enrages me more than it should—that tin ball

What a waste! I mutter
as I try to smooth it, as if I were patting my hair for
    a date

That was when I knew
I had turned into my Nana
a woman made up of wads of tissue, Ziploc bags &
    sheets of shiny foil
a rain bonnet in a foldable pouch
forever ready to reach inside
a drawer
or a pocket
or a sleeve
& retrieve what someone else needed
a way to stop a running nose
or a leaking eye
to keep the raindrops
from falling on your head
or carry a piece of found treasure
without tearing a hole in the seam of your pocket.
offering small bits of paper and cloth
not for her own nest
but someone else's.

I keep sheets of foil
to wrap over a late meal or
a slice of birthday cake
& packs of tissues to dab at the sadness
that sometimes leaks from us
& emergency plastic bags

to carry home
somethings found—
bits of sparkle
or the pieces of a broken heart

Maybe we all turn into my Nana
at some point
Maybe
it's not a bad thing.

THINGS THAT I HAVE GOOGLED...

What is the legal term when a wife kills her husband?

Bristol stool chart

Why are the lines on my chest so deep?

Help pooping

How to sleep better

Face yoga exercises for jowls

Does face yoga really work?

Why does Gen Z hate side parts?

Why do Gen Z hate portrait photos?

What is skibidi?

When does arthritis usually start?

How many years ago was 1992?

How old is Simon Le Bon?

Bar in West Village, downstairs, lights, 1980s?

love is not a
four-letter word

· · ·

The older I get, the more I say "I love you."

Not just to my family—I tell them I love them a hundred times a day. I tell them until they are sick of me, until they can predict what I am going to say before the words take leave from my tongue. I tell them so much and so often that now they say it back to me out of habit to get me to leave them alone.

Not just my family, though.

I sign off with love, with the abandon of an Oprah giveaway.

"Love you," I say at the end of phone calls to friends.

"Love you," I sign off on messages.

"Love you," I shout when I see them in person.

When I was younger, I kept those words close to my heart. I hoarded them. I suspect many of us did, hanging onto them and parsing them out only after careful consideration.

Does this person meet the requirements for my love? Do they tick all the boxes? Are they worthy of my love, of receiving those little words? All of those conditions that needed to be met, as if doling out love was a risk rather than a reward.

When I was younger, I was a love miser, a Valentine gal the color of Oscar the Grouch. I was stuffed with nonsense and misconceptions that love was only for swooning, that it should be saved for some Royal Charming who would eventually come along and sweep me up in a fairy tale cloud of carriage dust and whisk me away, or at the very least, ask me to dance during "Purple Rain."

I read too many magazine articles and took too many Cosmo quizzes.

How do you know if you really love him?

He loves me! He loves me not! Petals ripped from backyard daisies. He loves me not?

No love for you!

Older now, I throw the words about with abandon, spraying them like silly string until they form a sticky web that the people I love can't help but get caught up in. Snared by love.

Love you, friend.

I love the way you check in on me, and you, friend, who always has something nice to say, and you, over there? Love you, lady—thank you for the thoughtful gifts you always bring. I love you, friend, because you make me feel special when I'm around you, and you, because you always remind me of some bit of goodness in me that I sometimes have trouble seeing in myself.

I wish it hadn't taken me so long to realize that there is infinite room for love, that love doesn't have to be red roses and diamond rings, sworn vows, or forever-ever-afters.

Love is a moment or a lifetime, an act or a word, or something I haven't even thought of yet. It is birthday cakes and cups of cocoa, small smiles and impromptu calls. It is letters and cards and glances across the room. It's the smell of the sea on a walk with a friend, the glee of a reunion, and the ease of falling back into place.

I love you. I've been so stingy, treating love like a four-letter word.

Now I carry the syllables with me in my pockets, word confetti to shower down, settling like glitter on your shoulders.

I love you.

we can be heroes

· · ·

Ah, Gen X, the great unknown equation of a cohort—so unknown, in fact, that they slapped an algebraic placeholder on us and called it a day. We could have just as easily been Generation F for Forgotten or U for Unseen. The world shoved us through a screen door and told us not to come home until the porch light blinked on.

We're not perfect. The hairspray alone is responsible for a depleted chunk of ozone. Landfills are full of Gunny Sax taffeta prom dresses, polyester blends, and lots of single rhinestone gloves.

But...

We'd like, totally kick-ass in a crisis.

Nuclear event? Zombie invasion? Fungus among us? Generic catastrophe? Pfft. Not only did most of us watch *The Day After* and take notes, but we've also seen all the movies and shows in between. Yes, the neon was unfortunate and true, no one looked good in stirrup pants, but once you get past the surface stuff, it's easy to see how growing up in the '80s was really just a decade-long preparation for any apocalyptic scenario.

Need someone to sift through the rubble of atomic fallout or fend off brain-slurping, undead neighbors? We're your generation.

Always prepared for adventure

We *knew* tuning into *MacGyver* and *The A-Team* and watching them make explosives out of a shoe box, a bobby pin, and some baking soda would come in handy. How about opening tins with a twig or setting a successful trap with a sock and a prayer? I've seen *The Last of Us*—these are exactly the type of skills you'd need during a garden-variety apocalypse, never mind a mushroom zombie one. You're going to want that slightly graying Xer around in a crisis, trust me. Who else would be able to craft a splint out of a pen and a lint-coated piece of Hubba Bubba someone found at the bottom of a bag?

Strangers with nothing in common but each other

Everyone knows that in an apocalypse, you need a leader who is calm in a crisis. Endless and repeated viewings of 1980s movies with their easily recognizable archetypes make identifying leaders and delegating tasks as easy as falling off a log while you're practicing a dance at Kellerman's resort. Setting up a hierarchy of jocks, princesses, athletes, basket cases, and brains would be—well, a no-brainer. Need someone to build a radio out of scrap metal and a boom box antenna? Where's the brain? Need someone to use as bait to lure the zombies into a trap? Where's the James Spader bad boy character? The world has too many spoiled, rich White boys anyway. Here's their redemption arc.

Who needs a Molotov cocktail when you've got a can of Aqua Net?

If you ever did '80s hair, if you ever kept a can of Stiff Stuff in your locker for between-class touch-ups, or walked out of your room high on a funk of Aqua Net, you know the power of hairspray. If you ever had a girlfriend who used so much Rave that you could taste it over her Bonne Bell when you kissed her, you know how potent that power hold is. A can of Aqua Net and a cigarette lighter are all you need to keep the fungus from spreading or the zombies at bay.

Analog Life

We might be getting long in the tooth, but the fact that we lived half of our lives without modern tech is going to come in handy when the grids get blown, the cellular towers collapse, and your phone stops working. Seriously, our minds were blown by jack splitters and call waiting—it doesn't take much to impress us. But navigating a new landscape that probably looks a lot like the one from our childhoods means that while a group of young guns might struggle to find their way, not knowing how to navigate without a GPS or Google Maps, we Xers would know to hit the closest AAA supplier for an actual map. And we'd know how to read it. Bonus? We would be totally comfortable ringing someone's doorbell to ask directions.

Reality Bites

Back in the day, there were no reality television shows or YouTube clicks or TikTok endorsement deals for us. Even the game shows gave away washer and dryer sets, not cash. Our parents weren't arguing for better grades on our behalf; we were handed a set of keys at seven, and there were no cell phones to get us out of a jam. If your mom wasn't home to accept that collect call, you were stuck deciding whether or not to take a ride with that creepy neighbor who was trailing you in his IROC. We had to think on our feet on the playground. We had to call people on the phone and have face-to-face conversations. We had fistfights at three behind the gym. If anyone can navigate an unprecedented crisis, it's us.

Only boring people are bored

In between foraging for irradiated food or battles with the z'bies, there are bound to be long stretches of nothing to do but sit around. Gen X had 5 television channels. We had no internet. We had library books, a backyard, and parents who repeatedly told us that only boring people are bored. If we whined about it, they said, "I'll give you something to cry about," kicked us outside, and locked the screen door. We spent our entire childhoods, adolescence, and young adulthoods killing time; we can do it again. And if it gets really desperate, we can teach you how to make fart noises with your hands, fortune tellers out of paper, and the Hand Jive from *Grease*.

Clap on, clap off

Think of the confusion this could cause in a zombie situation. Lights on. Lights off. The undead wouldn't know if it was Night of the Living Dead, Day of the Living Dead, or what.

Pop Goes Perfection!

We had to solve a Rubik's Cube without the hacks. We had to do our research from the set of Encyclopedia Britannica in the library and footnote everything by hand. Figuring out what the next step in a dystopian setting is would be no big whoop for

Gen X. We honed our hand-eye coordination with Operation and learned to deal with anxiety by shoving plastic shapes into a board with a timer that ticked to the beat of angst. We got this.

Resilience

As a generation, we've seen our share of fads come...and go. If someone offers us a too-good-to-be-true device that can track zombie movement or detect fallout radiation, we're going to take them with a grain of MacGyver-made salt. Then we'll ask our resident Brain to just make one herself.

Crash Test Dummies

No seatbelts, no worries. Our teenage friends used to ride around in Jeeps with no roofs. We're used to using ingenuity to get from Point A to Point B. We know how to ride in the way back and would seamlessly transition to more unorthodox methods of transportation to outrun zombies or ash clouds: roller skates, Big Wheels, Huffies, and BMX racers. Hippity hops and pogo sticks, and if there's a snowy hill nearby? We'd grab a saucer sled and go.

Very Special Episodes

Don't be surprised at just how much we picked up watching ABC Afterschool Specials. You really don't know when being able to spot which survivor is suffering from an eating disorder, who came from a divorced family, or whose dad was a secret alcoholic might come in handy. Knowledge is power, people. Knowledge is power.

I've had the time of my life

Look, we've all seen the movies. Not everyone is going to survive the apocalypse. I like to think that if any Xers were minutes away from being caught by a zombie mob and having our brains sucked out of our eye sockets, infested by a mushroom, or indeed, engulfed by a mushroom cloud, we'd try to go out in style. Give us a hot second, and we'll commandeer a parade float and sing "Danke Schoen" at full volume. Maybe perform a previously impossible lift at the end of a dance routine or reinvent ourselves as a Dread Pirate. We'll cycle across the moon or dance with an undead throng a la Thriller.

And if all else fails?

We'll just say no.

here you come again

. . .

If I could peer into my kitchen future, an All-Clad saucepan lid as my scrying mirror, the sight of carrots left to peel and dinners left to plan would probably make me sink to the white tile floor in despair. Nevertheless, I julienne.

When I'm feeling particularly ornery about the whole prospect—often—or when I know I'm going to be on my feet for a while—also, often—I put on a carefully curated playlist I call Kitchen Bitch. The name is a tribute to the wonderfully grumpy Greek woman who once served us breakfast on holiday in Rhodes. Each day, she shuffled into the breakfast room in her plastic slippers and slammed a pot of coffee on the table with enough force to shake the cutlery. She never smiled. Not once in a week. She'd leave the coffee, fling some plasticky-looking ham at us, and shuffle off, her plastic slippers slap, slap, slapping on the floor.

One morning toward the end of our stay, she appeared in a black T-shirt. Across her ample, middle-aged bosom, white letters spelled out *Kitchen Bitch*. Around bites of our plastic-y ham and sips of coffee, we wondered whether it was a gift from a bemused customer, if she wore it with knowing irony, or if she just pulled the nearest piece of clean clothing off the chair to go and serve processed meat to a room full of sunburned tourists.

I can't tell you how many times I have thought about that shirt in the decades since, or how many times I've felt like nothing more than a kitchen bitch myself—slave to the constant culinary needs of my family.

I'm not enough of a music aficionado to call the playlist eclectic—but let's call it a mixtape of tunes that are pleasing to chop and mince to. Sometimes, my husband will come home and find me playing the air trumpet to "Mambo No. 5" while I wait for a pot to boil; sometimes, a child finds me chopping onions to the beat of The Violent Femmes. There's no reason, but plenty of musical rhyme—everything from The Communards to Carly Simon, Duran Duran to Dolly Parton.

Wait—did I tell you that until I turned fifty, I avoided Dolly Parton like the plague?

If I had a cultural Rubicon, Dolly Parton was it.

I WAS ten when *9 to 5* came out on the big screen, and while I can't imagine that my parents took me to see it in the theater with baggies of Jiffy Pop, it's possible. The late '70s and early '80s were wild.

If I tumbled out of bed and stumbled to the kitchen today, I'd tell you that *9 to 5* was an overlooked moment of feminist cinema history, but back then? It wasn't cups of ambition as much as bra cups overflowing with boob jokes.

Though Parton had already made her name as a country crooner by the time *9 to 5* hit the theaters, her turn as the bodacious Doralee is my first real memory of her. That role was followed by one in *The Best Little Whorehouse in Texas,* in which she played a bawdy bordello madam in a musical about sex workers.

Truly, when I tell you that Gen X was born into some nutsy times, I'm not lying.

I was vaguely aware of Parton after that—mostly as a variety show and late-night talk show guest, but I was growing up in the Northeast US, solid blue Yankee country. My parents didn't listen to country music. No one I knew listened to country music. Country music, as far as my young, unseasoned self was concerned, was for Southerners and people with names like Jeb or Dixie.

Oh, we all watched *The Dukes of Hazzard*. The girls were sweet on Bo and Luke, and I'm sure the boys lusted over Catherine Bach in her Daisy Dukes, but the South was as foreign a place to me as the moon. The Mason-Dixon line isn't just a physical border that separates North and South in the US; it's a cultural and psychological border as well, perhaps even more so.

Living north of that invisible line influenced my feelings about the South, country music, grits, and, of course, Dolly Parton.

ON TALK SHOWS or variety performances, Parton leaned *hard* into the dumb blonde jokes and double D entendres. She leaned in so hard that it seemed like the jokes went right over her head, as if she were unaware of the sexual innuendo flying fast and loose around her.

The only thing worse than the male hosts taking cheap shots while ogling her bustline was watching *her* make jokes at her own expense. Even as a kid, it felt wrong. It left me with a nasty taste in my mouth, a thin coat of sexualized grime on my brain.

In my small New England town, I was busy going from an awkward, somewhat impressionable tween to a still awkward, somewhat mouthy diet goth. Parton popped up here and there, always in something low-cut, blonde curls cascading down her back. She sang sappy duets with Kenny Rogers that crossed over into mainstream top 40 charts. There were Hallmark movies and Christmas movies. In all of them, the punchline was her bustline.

Dolly Parton was everything I was not. She was tiny and buxom and so southern I could taste honeysuckle on my tongue whenever I heard her speak. I was tall and skinny, trying to get out of a small Jack & Diane town and run off to the city. More than the differences in the way we looked and spoke, more than the geographical and cultural chasm that separated us, Dolly seemed to be the embodiment of everything I didn't want to be.

I was smart—my teachers knew it, but more importantly, I knew it. And I was growing up in an era when it was ok to acknowledge my intelligence. No hiding my smarts behind eyelash flutters or getting the math problem wrong to spare the feelings of Craig of the Blond Hair. Girls were going to college to get more knowledge. Women were working, bringing home bacon hidden in their massive shoulder pads. Helen Reddy roared from the car radio. Well, okay, she sang, but she sang about roaring.

That was what I wanted for myself. I wanted to get by on my brains, not my boobs. To a young me, Dolly Parton was nothing more than a sad joke. Her blondness, her breast size, and her twangy, southern-fried voice. She was a walking, talking caricature of the dumb blonde—the one that the men I knew liked to laugh at.

I wanted nothing to do with that; I thought I was better than that.

I felt bad for her.

OH, hindsight, you fickle beast. It would take me years and college courses and, most of all, a life lived rather than imagined to understand that what was happening to Parton's *9-to-5* character on screen was happening to girls and women in real life.

And it didn't matter what size bra you wore. It didn't matter if you were blonde or brunette, short or tall, or if you liked Poison or Johnny Cash.

That Parton made a movie about sexual harassment at a time when there wasn't even a name for sexual harassment went right over my head.

In the '80s I grew up in, high school girls were a commodity that high school boys tore through like a pack of Big Red gum. If you were lucky, no one called you a slut in public, even if all you'd ever done was let Danny Simpson cop a feel over your shirt at some basement party with stale beer and a tinfoil bong.

If you were lucky, it was just your heart that got broken and not your nose or an arm. Sometimes, when I think back to the girls I knew who got hurt by the boys I knew, I want to weep with rage.

It didn't matter if you were a cheerleader, a party girl, or class president; despite Helen Reddy and the shoulder pads, we were all still girls in a world set up for boys. I thought smart girls could get ahead with nothing but their brains. Funny story—it turns out that even when we do, we're *still* accused of getting ahead with our magical vaginas.

I spent more than a few midnights leaning forward on city bar tops, exposing maximum cleavage to get the bartender's attention, yet it never occurred to me that I was doing exactly what I had judged Parton so harshly for doing. It was a long time before I recognized that most women use their bodies as currency at one point or another, even if it's only to get their drink faster. Often, it's the only currency we're allowed to keep in our pockets.

The '80s morphed into the '90s. Grunge came and went. An array of nameless, faceless bands that all looked and sounded the same in the early noughties. In the intervening decades, I was falling off barstools and battling depression. I met the right guy, fell in love, had kids, and mourned the death of my father. I moved across the ocean, then another one. I spent a lot of years and tears trying to figure out how the hell I—Dina of the big brain and the big dreams—ended up as a housewife.

Throughout all of this, Parton remained on the periphery, fading in and out of the spotlight. But I was too busy raising a family and parsing through my own mental chaos to give the Smoky Mountain Songstress much thought.

Until 2020, the year the world went into lockdown.

That's when I started to notice something odd.

Dolly Parton was *everywhere*.

She was the subject of an array of podcasts. Scholars were analyzing the feminist—or anti-feminist—messages of "Jolene." At the University of Tennessee, Knoxville, there was an honors history class called "Dolly's America." Her philanthropy, long under the radar, was coming to light. The millions of books she had donated to underprivileged kids and the donation to the Covid vaccine.

Wait...what? The Covid vaccine?

That one caught my interest, and from there, it was a melodic slide down the Dollywood-themed rabbit hole. The more I learned about Dolly Parton, the more I was forced to reconsider and reorganize my thoughts—not just about her, but about myself.

While I was in the kitchen chopping onions and salting the pasta water, I listened to a podcast about Parton's early career. The irony was as pungent as the garlic. The math I was so proud of acing in sixth grade? It got me nowhere. It didn't even help me remember how to convert ounces to grams. In between the slicing and the dicing, there were a lot of uncomfortable realizations—about my view of success, value, how those things are defined, and just who gets to do the defining.

It wasn't just the onions making me teary.

· · ·

When I was young and thought I knew everything there was to know, I saw Dolly Parton as a sell-out. I thought she had cheapened her worth to sell some records. But worse than that, it felt to me like she had sold out women everywhere by relying on her body to do it.

Over a pile of neatly diced vegetables, I listened to Parton's stories of starting out in the business, of the way she was perceived, of the harassment she endured, and of how she eventually came to leverage all of that in her favor. Far from being taken advantage of, Parton's decision to exploit her bodily assets to boost her financial assets was a calculated one. Dolly wasn't just in on the joke; she was making money off of it.

The joke was never on her. The joke was on me.

Here she comes again, a woman in an industry dominated by exploitation and masculinity, a woman who looked around and said, *No matter what I do, this is what they're going to see. The only thing I can do is figure out how I can use that to my advantage.* Then she hiked up her substantial brassiere and got on with it.

Even as a young woman just starting out, Parton was smart enough to understand what she needed to do to succeed in a world that is almost always hellbent on stopping women like Dolly Parton from getting ahead. Not just because she's blonde, but because she's tiny and Southern and female and blonde. She grew up dirt poor in Appalachia, living for a time in a one-room cabin. She was never meant to succeed; every deck was stacked against her.

So she bought her own deck and went all in.

I used to feel sorry for Dolly Parton because she never stood up to people who were making jokes at her expense. Meanwhile, she was laughing all the way to the bank. She rode those jokes into a position of control until she could do what she wanted, including quietly helping her community and funding vaccines.

If being an independent woman was my goal, it's hard to think of a better role model.

And I had dismissed her completely.

ONE OF THE less pleasant aspects of getting on in years is discovering all the ways in which my younger self was an asshole. At the same time, those same realizations can be the most rewarding ones. Looking at things from a new angle might prove that yes, you were wrong, or yes, you were a biased butthead, but if you pay attention to what you were missing, you might find something worthwhile.

Which is how I ended up chopping carrots, singing along to "Islands in the Stream" on a playlist called Kitchen Bitch. Sometimes, I wonder if the grumpy old Greek woman in her ironic tee was slapping coffee down in the mornings and walking to the bank in the afternoons with the day's profits from a hotel she owned.

Maybe she had another T-shirt that said *Boss Bitch*.

I hope so.

I also know what my next playlist is going to be called.

playlist

Kitchen Bitch

through the looking glass, down the rabbit hole

. . .

I've lost count of the times I have lain in bed, tossing, turning, and throwing the covers off and then on again while trying desperately to slide into sleep. I listen to the noises of the city night, the snaky hiss of car tires on wet concrete outside, a faraway argument. I listen to the soft noises of the darkness around me. My husband's breathing, slow and steady. The low hum of the refrigerator. I count backward by threes from five hundred. I turn onto my back, like a turtle. I turn onto my stomach, like a slug. I flip and I flop like a fish gasping for breath until I finally lie still, stare up at the ceiling, and give in.

It's my brain that betrays me in these moments of darkness. Not by trying to puzzle out something important, but by insisting that midnight moment is the time to remember some arcane piece of information from my past. A television episode. A middle school event. A boy I kissed in my early twenties, or a bar I went to when I lived in New York. A snippet of a song or melody lodged in my cerebral cortex.

Once, there was a tune that started in the middle of the night and stayed in my head into the morning, whining like a mosquito near my ear. Convinced it was something important, I called my husband and tried to get him to hear what was going around and around in my head by humming into the phone, only for him to identify it as the theme tune to *Shaun the Sheep*.

Another time, I spent hours on Google Maps looking for the name of a dive bar I used to go to when I was just another girl trying to sneak into dank basement establishments with a dodgy fake ID. I knew vaguely where it was—West Village—and I could remember what it looked like—steps leading down into the bar, dim purple and blue lighting. I knew I used to tease my hair and drink cheap well vodka drinks, because that's what I did once upon a misspent youth. For the life of me, I could not remember the name of the place.

It took hours of searching, half a day lost to some random memory that could have been used for something else. There was no rhyme or reason to it all; nothing significant happened at this bar. I went there a handful of times, overteased and over made-up, desperate to feel cool. There was no reason why I needed to remember the name, yet the memory was stuck in my brain like a popcorn kernel. I kept working at it with my tongue, shoving it deeper and deeper into my memories.

If nothing else, finally tracking it down dislodged the memory and gave me a moment of relief.

This is what happens to me now in my fifties. A vague wisp of a memory, a fleeting thought, and then far too much time spent chasing down ghosts of the past.

I RAN across something on the internet about looking for something—probably a charger cable; they always seem to go missing—and ending up surrounded by photo albums on the kitchen floor hours later, weeping. I'd never felt so seen, like the Goddess of Chaotic Organizers was peering into my soul.

The number of times I've started to clean out a closet or a

drawer and pulled a ticket stub out of a coat I haven't worn for ten years and ended up down a rabbit hole, chasing some memory? Many. A photo of something—you can't remember what exactly—triggers a different memory, one that requires that you call your high school friend, the one with the memory like a steel trap, to see if you're remembering real life or an episode of *Growing Pains*. By the time you surface, it's time to make dinner, and the contents of your closet or the kitchen drawers are still strewn around.

Alice Through the Looking Glass, only Alice is not nearly as young as she used to be, has to squeeze her middle-aged ass through, and it takes a lot more time to travel back from those trips down memory lane.

I swear, sometimes I get jet lag.

Is THERE a name for the creep of nostalgia that starts to happen in your forties? By the time you hit mid-century Danish design stride, it's in full swing. The clothes you wore in high school have done another round in fashion, and the bands you listened to—once cool, then uncool—are now old enough to be *retro cool,* and they're limping onto festival stages, all knee replacements and Botoxed eyebrows, making them look as surprised as you are at just how they got there.

When you're here, on the flip side of fifty, the past gets viewed through a prism rather than a microscope. There is simply too much stuff to remember. Remembering who left what, where, and passport expiration dates, and if I've called my mother recently. Birthdays and preferences and deadlines and payments. Strings of numbers and passwords that require an unholy trinity of capital letters, numbers, and symbols.

My brain is overflowing, a tub with the taps left on, memories seeping into the cracks of the hardwood and into the crawl-space between ceiling and floor.

I've lost most of my high school years. Not just the day-to-day stuff, like what class I had 7th period or where I sat for lunch, but big stuff—it feels like I should be able to remember it, tease it out from the hippocampus. Josh, who ran away and was later found in another state, and a classmate who had a child while we were still in school. Friends with better memories bring these things up when we are together. Sometimes, with the context clues, I can dig back through my mind, a memory archaeologist, and piece together events into something whole. I've forgotten whole people, people who walked the same hallways and sat on the same orange button cafeteria stools.

The lyrics to "Total Eclipse of the Heart"? No problem. The exact words that asshole Bobby Vegara said to me in 8th grade? Seared into memory. But other things, big things that feel important enough to remember, are not where they should be.

Much like the charging cables.

Sometimes, my memory likes to torture me with memories that I'd prefer to keep buried. Embarrassing hookups, questionable choices. There they stay, not lodged but loose and limber, dancing around in my head as I stare up at the ceiling, trying to figure out why they decided to re-emerge.

Sometimes it's a name, seemingly out of nowhere. Many times, events that I feel are connected but are missing the thing that links them, some footbridge lost to the mists of time and alcohol.

I spend far too much time and mental energy chasing these things down, searching for rabbits with pocket watches, and ending up at tea parties I don't want to be at.

I expected that as I got older and my brain files got full to the point of bursting, there would be gold medal moments that stood on the mantlepiece of memory, polished and bright. Instead, the whole surface seems to be taken up with random remembrance knick-knacks that have no use other than as dust collectors.

If only we could Marie Kondo our memories. Does this one bring you joy? No? You are the weakest link. Goodbye.

Down the rabbit hole, through the looking glass. Mad Hatters, and there was once a guy who smiled like a Cheshire Cat; I think it was at a bar in the West Village. Ah, yes. That's how I got here, here being a random hour of darkness when I should be sleeping. Scroll, rewind, and chase it down to make sure it's real.

Was that me... Or was it Jan Brady? Tomorrow I'll call Diane and ask her; maybe Joanne kept it in her box of blackmail memorabilia.

Sometimes, when I've given up trying to pry a memory from the depths of my half-consciousness, I wonder if there are others doing the same. Do I wander, ghost-like, through someone else's memories while they search for a name in the quiet of the night? We all have stories of random meetings, of kids from grade school whose names have stuck with us for no reason. Does Craig of the Blond Hair have the shape of a random girl in his fourth-grade class that haunts him? Is there someone out there, lying awake at two am, trying to remember the name of that girl dressed in secretarial cosplay, second row from the back, in their 2nd grade class picture? Is there a man, jolting awake in the dark of the night, his partner softly breathing beside him, thinking about a girl he kissed once in a dark bar back in the late '80s?

What *was* her name?

Dina.

And it was probably at the Scrap Bar.

coffee in bed

. . .

Years ago, there was a rumor that I brought my husband coffee in bed every morning. The wives and mothers I shared my days with rolled their eyes at me and said things like, "Please, tell us this isn't true!" and "Now my husband is going to want coffee in bed!" And, of course, "You know they all think coffee in bed is a euphemism for something else, right?"

In an effort to set the record straight, I addressed the rumor head-on.

Except it wasn't really a rumor. The truth is that I did bring my husband coffee in bed every morning.

I LIKED to say that coffee in bed was payment in kind. You see, I used to have a bad habit of blaming my husband for all the things I tend to misplace throughout the course of my life. My bag, a pair of shoes, an important piece of something I need. My sanity. I used to lose my phone almost daily. Once, when the children were young and I was rushing to get them to school and couldn't find whatever it was I needed, he stood there, watching me hurl coats off the rack and shoes out of the basket, and calmly said, "You're going to blame me for this, aren't you?"

"Yes!" I yelled at him. "Even though I know it's not your fault, I will! I will totally, totally blame you!"

I used to blame him when I got lost or when he could not immediately pinpoint my location from my frantic woman-on-the-street descriptions. *There's a building! A store. No, I don't know what the street sign says!* I am a terrible map reader, and I used to panic when I didn't know where I was or where I was going. For a long time, I expected that my husband, the man who vowed to love me in sickness and in health, in lost and in found, could get me home. That if necessary, he would extract me SWAT-style from whatever map-challenged predicament I'd gotten myself into.

He was my knight in Google Maps armor.

So I brought him coffee in bed every morning.

That's not actually why I brought him coffee. I brought him coffee because he is categorically *not* a morning person. To have him underfoot in the a.m. would have caused, in the parlance of Thomas the Tank Engine, confusion and delay. He would be grumpy and in everyone's way, and we would all suffer.

I did it for the sake of the children.

No, not really.

I brought him coffee because he puts the pillowcases on because he knows how much I hate putting the pillowcases on. He scrubs the bathroom because he knows if he left it up to me, it wouldn't get done. I make sure his family gets birthday cards for the same reason. I do the school stuff; he does the camping stuff. While I break out in hives at the very idea of fishing and cooking over an open flame, he has the same histamine reaction to the idea of small talk with people at school open houses.

So I brought him coffee.

Back when I was young and idealistic, I thought the quickest way to equality was splitting things down the middle. Make a giant list of all the things in life that need doing and then just cleave it in half. You take the left, I'll take the right, and everyone is happy. I read once about marital contracts—pieces of signed paper that spelled out who was responsible for what. If it's Tuesday, it's your turn to vacuum, and if it's Friday, it must be my turn to cook.

Then I grew up.

I got married and had kids. For a while, I hung on to my half-a-contract notion of equality, but all I got in return was seething resentment. It infuriated me that it never seemed to be fair, that I was always doing more of the things that no one wanted to do. If my husband changed one diaper, I changed 284. When our children were tiny, one would wake from a nightmare and call out for "Daddy," who would be snoring next to me while I steamed at the gall of the universe for making me get out of a warm, cozy bed when *his* child had clearly voiced a preference.

You can have a contract that is signed, sealed, and delivered to your house by an attorney in a gorilla suit. You can laminate it and nail it to the door like Luther's treatise—or, barring that, on the family bulletin board. You can memorize it, put it to music, and copyright the damn thing, and *none* of that will ease the fury when Wednesday rolls around and your partner doesn't vacuum even though it's *clearly* their turn, and there is an army of dust bunnies getting ready to reenact the charge of the dust brigade.

Even if it's written in blood that "thou shalt not blame your spouse when you misplace your keys," I can almost guarantee you're still going to do it. Even if you only do it in your head.

It took me a long time to realize something obvious about relationships, raising kids, and life in general: it is never fair, and it's never equal. You love each other, and you hurt each other, and you argue over who left the toothpaste to harden like mortar on the side of the sink. You live and you learn, and you stare at each other over the beautiful mess of a life and thank the universe for sending you this person, because who else would put up with the moods or the morning breath? Who else is going to let you squeeze their blackheads or remind you when Mother's Day is every year? Who else is going to remember that you hate putting the pillowcases on or that you need an extraordinary amount of time to wake up in the morning?

I put up with his schizo Gemini moods, and he pretends he doesn't mind when we have crackers and cheese for dinner.

If love and marriage go together like a horse and carriage, then compromise and understanding are the whip and driver that get it moving.

When the kids were young, mornings often brought chaos and disillusionment with life. When there was a stopwatch counting down the lunches to be made, shoes tied, and getting everyone out the door in a reasonable fashion—ready, set, go!—I often used the quiet of that early morning hour to collect my thoughts.

I would get up and make a pot of coffee while I was pottering and slapping peanut butter on slices of bread, often still yawning the night away. It never occurred to me not to bring my husband a cup of coffee or to demand that he join me in the kitchen while I silently padded from refrigerator to sink, making mental lists and trying to remember the last time I changed the pillowcases.

I brought him coffee because I was making it anyway. It was a small act of kindness, a cup of caffeinated care. As I used to tell our kids all the time, kindness doesn't cost you anything most of the time.

Maybe those small acts of kindness, the ones that don't cost you anything, are the pothole fillers that help smooth out the road so that we can all get where we are going in one, unbroken piece.

Now the kids are grown, and the mornings are far less hectic. The alarms aren't set so early, and there are no sports matches to rush to on a Saturday morning. We have a fancier coffee machine that only requires me to push a button and wait. Now that his presence in the kitchen wouldn't cause such confusion and delay, do I still bring him a coffee?

I do—at least Monday through Friday.

The weekends? Even though it was never in any marital contract or signed in coffee grounds, it's me who gets coffee in bed. *

---

* It's still not a euphemism...

interlude

Oh, perchance to dream
thru starburst nights--if only
I could freaking sleep

_____

beat the traffic

. . .

Why do we pause to take stock at thirty, forty, or fifty? Why not at twenty-seven or thirty-two or forty-six? Surely, the highway of self-reflection would be less jammed with head-scratching fifty-year-olds in a pile-up, all trying to figure out how we got here?

We should all try harder to beat the self-reflection traffic.

What's left to reflect on anyway? I've spent so much time on this Isle of Me. I know the atlas of myself with my eyes closed, and it's folded like one of those AAA maps that used to get you to Aunt Janice's house and back. I know the topography: the mountains that have eroded and the plains that have expanded. I've been there for all of them, responsible for most. I can free-solo the mountain of my anxieties without a safety net, with nothing but a manky bandaid in my pocket. I can plumb the murky depths of my emotions, knowing when to surface without getting the bends from spending too much time in the deep water of the past.

Truly, how much more self-reflection is expected here?

Should I expect more? Because if so, I want to plan ahead and beat the traffic.

this is a love song

. . .

Some say that into every generation, a slayer is born. I am not her.

I am not brave enough or fit enough, nor do I have the hand-eye coordination needed to wield a sharp stick. Hell, I've hurt myself with a vegetable peeler; I am definitely not a slayer born.

What I *am* is a mixtape of memories, feelings, emotions, and recollections. I'm also of an age when all of those things start to collide with my day-to-day life. The memories butt up against the way I parent. The recollections color the way I love. The feelings and emotions chafe against the way I see the world.

It's almost impossible not to compare the world we're living in with the one I grew up in. My brain automatically sifts things into color-coded and tabbed lists of pros and cons, befores and afters, and betters and worsers.

This isn't about who walked up the longer hill in deeper snow or knew the value of hard work, though.

This?

Let's call it a love song dedicated to a firefly generation.

I SEE YOU, my fellow children of the Walkman, those of us who grew up terrified of summer camps on lakes and nuclear apocalypses in equal measure, who looked—and acted—thirty by the time we were fifteen.

This is a love song to feet upon the door jambs, the phone cord winding from toe to thigh, for handheld tape recorders, boom boxes, and the small thrill of hitting Record at the perfect moment.

A song born of seesaw thumps and unscheduled summer days, of boredom and stacks of hardcover books with crinkly cellophane covers from the town library, of daydreams and catching fireflies in jars, of skinned knees that stung and fizzed under a shower of hydrogen peroxide.

To the pleasure of Nancy Drew-ing your way through the song clues of a mixtape, *does this mean he likes me*?! To brown paper bag book covers tattooed with band names and denim jackets heavy with pins; to ribbon barrettes and side ponytails and Goody combs in your back pocket.

This is a love song to roller skating in cul-de-sacs and handlebar streamers flying in the wind, to BMX bandits and pink Huffy girls. To chocolate trails of Reese's Pieces just in case extraterrestrials were real, to treasure hunts in the woods, and the sound of a Coke can kicked with force, olly olly oxen free.

My mother and your mother were hanging out the clothes. Your mother wears combat boots; mine has silver buttons all down her back, back, back. One banana, two banana, three banana, four.

To backyard campouts with bags of melted marshmallows and plastic lounge chairs that left marks on your skin like lashes.

This is a poem to Orange Julius and Spencer Gifts, to Fiorenza and Jessica McClintock. To Aqua Net and Stiff Stuff,

Le Disc, FotoMat, and Bonne Belle. For ten packs of Life Savers that opened like a book.

To the bottoms of feet toughened from walking over hot asphalt driveways and hours jumping through the sprinkler arc. To slip 'n slides and hose water and lawn darts that could kill you.

This is a love song to magic, to stories, and possibility. To the gilt edges of Encyclopedia Britannica and the musty smell of card catalogs, book fairs, and Dynamite magazine.

Miss Lucy had a baby and named it Tiny Tim she put him on the engine, engine number nine. Do you want your money back? Oh, yeah.

Sunday, Monday, happy days spent waiting, not for Godot, but for the end of the school day, summer, sweet sixteens, and a boy whose initials you could write in the middle of a chalk heart.

4eva.

These were the days of our lives.

THIS IS AN ODE TO WAITING—FOR the crush to call, for film to be developed, for college acceptance letters and SAT scores, and for pen pal letters with loopy handwritten swirls. For your favorite show to return, for the commercials to end, to see if Mom or Dad would collect you from the cot in the nurse's office or if you'd just puke and go back to class.

A song sung to the scent of freshly mimeographed paper and purple fingerprints. To scratchy film reels and boxy television sets wheeled into class, to sitting in the dark of Western Civ. and doodling in the margins of your textbook.

To textbooks.

This is a love song about whole days trying to swing over the bar while two friends held down the frame to make sure it didn't pull all the way up from the ground. To flying off midair and the jar in your ankles that went straight up to your chin. To the permanent bump on the inside of your middle finger. To curlicue Ds and serpentine Ss.

To the clack, clack, swipe of typewriters and the hum of busy signals, to modem screeches and hours spent programming just to watch your name loop in green letters on a black computer screen. To road trips stretched out on the backseat and bruised hipbones from bouncing around in the flatbed of a neighbor's Ford.

To my bologna's first name and last, to commercial tunes that still earworm their way through your cerebral cortex well into middle age. Monchichi, Monchichi, oh so soft and two all-beef patties, special sauce, lettuce, cheese—gee whiz, I don't want to grow up, because, baby, if I did.

This is a poem to the smell of Noxema, Hawaiian Tropic, and Ogilvy perms. To date stamps in books. To the delicate wings of corsage petals pressed in the dictionary under L for love.

This is an ode to the perfect feathered bang and to Ponyboy Curtis. To Wolverines and Goonies, Kellerman's Lodge and Rydell High. To hand-jives and pachangas, footloose and fancy-free. As you wish.

I mean it. Anybody got a peanut?

To hours spent on a friend's bedroom shag carpeting listening to records. To Freckle Juice and Margaret and Deenie, to mothers who refused to answer the phone when General Hospital was on.

To freedom, when roaming was by foot and not by cellular plan, and you could figure things out and make mistakes without the world watching on. When you could put a key in the door and walk into a never-ending story, or hide in a closet and pretend it was Narnia, where, in the space of an afternoon, anything seemed possible.

This is for after-school specials and summer ice cream cones, cannonballs and sandcastles, shouts of "Marco" followed by a chorus of "Polos," for Tiger Beat and neon and purple acid-washed rain. Pennies taped to the record needle and double albums with the lyrics inside. To parachute pants that swished when you walked, wallet chains, and dates at Pizza Hut.

It's a song of sick days under the afghan your Auntie Kathy made with a sleeve of saltines, flat ginger ale, and The Price is Right. Come on down! Or the thrill on a snowy morning of hearing your school's name on the radio.

Here's to measuring maturity by the television shows you were allowed to stay up and watch on Saturday nights. Come aboard, we're expecting you. To gravity-defying hair and blue eyeshadow the color of a perfect sky. To metalheads and goth girls and freaks and geeks and all the ones who didn't fit in when fitting in was the only thing that mattered.

To the perfect song at the end of a perfect movie that defined a generation they couldn't define.

They tried anyway.

A basket case. A brain. An athlete. A princess. A criminal.

This is a love song for us all.

SADD
Students
Against
Drunk
Driving

The
"New Haw
Times"
Staff

SAYINGS:
NoWell, Maybe
Dont be a receptor
Wicked Awesome WENCH
NoProblem! E-YA
No Boot
Oh ya

YaRight!

Just
Say
No!

Concerts
Beach
Shopping

1988

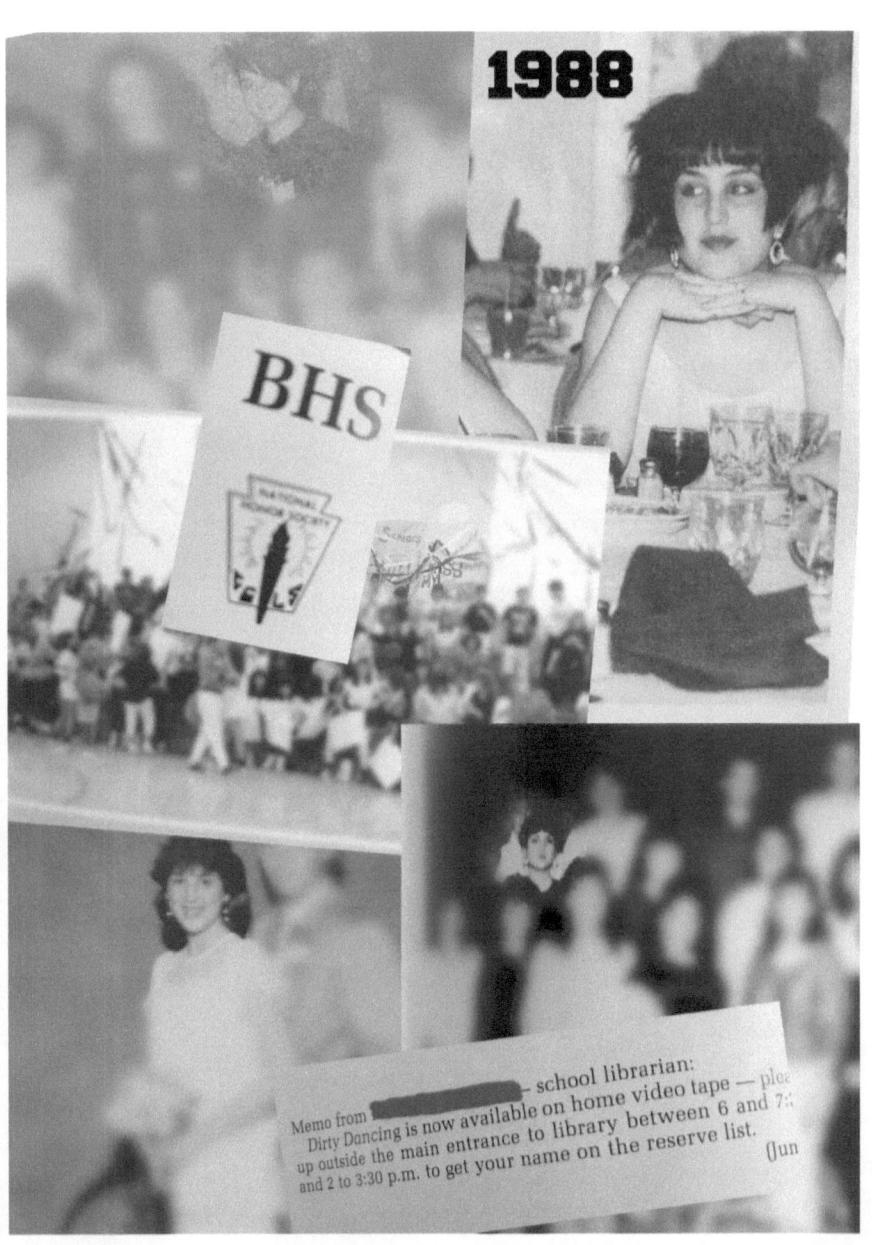

1988

BHS

Memo from ▬▬▬▬▬ – school librarian:
Dirty Dancing is now available on home video tape — plea
up outside the main entrance to library between 6 and 7:
and 2 to 3:30 p.m. to get your name on the reserve list.   Jun

stop all the clocks

. . .

When I was eight months pregnant with my first son, my father turned yellow. It was the day of my baby shower. I remember it clearly: the sunshiny tint of his skin, the way the whites of his eyes looked vaguely wolfish. Clearly, something was not right.

Jaundice, we thought.

Cancer, they said.

The doctors fixed the yellow but not the cancer. They gave him less than a year to live, and they were right; he died nine months after my son was born. It was three months after his sixtieth birthday, a birthday not all that far off from where I am now. So close I don't even have to put on my glasses to see it looming on the horizon.

The number sixty blinks a neon beat in my head, like a personal doomsday clock. Most of the time, it silently measures the weeks, the months, the years. Other times, usually in the pitch black of a pre-dawn day, it's as loud as church bells in my skull.

When I was young, sixty seemed ancient. I was just shy of thirty-five when my father died, and even then, sixty seemed a distant shore, one I had to shield my eyes with the ridge of my palm to see. Now that it's within striking distance, it hardly seems like a moment since I was in high school studying for a chemistry test or sitting up in the soft dark of night rocking an infant to sleep.

Time is funny like that; it just disappears.

If energy is never created or destroyed, what about time? What happens with the minutes and months we waste? I try to hoard time, stuff it in my cheeks and my pockets, but it just evaporates from where I try to keep it in a lid with the jar screwed tight.

Nine to twelve months.

Sixty years, three months, twenty-nine days. It hardly seems like a lot.

Once you have a countdown, everything is stained by the idea of last. Strawberry blotched and livid.

FOUR MONTHS BEFORE HE DIED, we were at an old, falling-down house my husband and I had bought, excited about fixing it up. I hugged him, commenting on how bumpy he was, swallowing the lump in my own throat to get the joke out. He loved a joke, my father. "Those are the tumors," he told me with a wry grin. I swallowed the terror to avoid freaking out.

I freaked out anyway.

Are you ok? I asked constantly, bringing him an extra blanket, a cup of tea. I'm sure he thought I meant, Are you in any pain? Does anything hurt? Do you need anything from me?

What I really meant was, how does it feel to know that you are dying?

We're all dying, of course; every day we're dying, and cells are suiciding, shutting down, and taking off for greener pastures. Going wherever it is that time goes when it is spent. My collagen cells hung up a retirement shingle long ago, and I don't think they're ever coming back, not even to visit.

But to know that you are actively dying, that in one month or three or six you will be gone?

I could not wrap my head around the idea. I still can't.

"I've had a good life," my father said to me, and I nodded back at him. But I wanted more answers.

Was it long enough? Was it warm enough? Did you do enough, love enough, see enough? Was it enough?

I am haunted by the word.

Enough.

It is arbitrary and made up, and there is no heavenly scale or earthly one that is going to weigh whether you've done or been or seen or loved enough. No one wants to stand, anxious and unsure if they end up in some form of an afterlife while Anubis weighs their heart to see if it was enough.

There's something in me that wants to be sure, though, sure that I've done enough. But when I try to define what *enough* means, it escapes, a dragonfly of a thought let loose into a cloudless sky.

Not that long ago, I was fifty, and in not too much time, I'll be fifty-five, and life has been lived, and love has taken root and burrowed further into the soil of my being, and so much has happened, but is it *enough*?

Have I done enough?

There are times when I lie in bed at night next to my slumbering spouse, staring at the ceiling, trying to suck enough air into my lungs to breathe. The weight of time is so heavy on my chest that I feel like I am suffocating. In those moments of inky blackness, I feel utterly alone, caught in a web of my own making. Sometimes I think of my father. I think of my mother, who is marching ever faster toward some sort of ending, who even now, at eighty, feels like it hasn't been enough. When we speak, I listen to her recite a litany of names of the dead. The names don't interest me. I don't write that to sound callous; each of those names held a life, the letters of their names bookends to birth and death. Their loved ones will feel the absence of their laughter.

But in those moments, I am selfish.

I breathe and count backwards. You still have nine years before you reach sixty. You have eight years before you reach sixty. You have seven, six, five years before you reach sixty. That's a lot of time; you can chip away at *enough*.

Will it ever be enough?

I want to stop the clocks—not forever, just long enough to catch my breath, to make a plan, to get in shape, to lose ten pounds, to go to the dentist like I've been putting off, and get that stupid implant, cost be damned. Long enough to make sure my kids know what they need to know, to claw back the hours I've wasted on social media looking at cats and worrying about the wrong things. To write more and love more and cook less.

Stop all the clocks. I want time to think without the constant tick, tick, tick that runs like a metronome echo in the back of my mind.

I've had a good life, my father said to me that day. In between those words, I think he was letting me know that he was not afraid of dying.

I don't know if the words were true. What I think is that those five words were the only gift he could give me to take forward.

I've had a good life.

If I could stop all the clocks, just long enough to go back to that day, his blue eyes looking into my brown ones, I would be brave enough to ask him what I really wanted to ask. I would not tap dance around the question like a vaudevillian.

Has it been enough?

Time marches by, the tempo increasing with each year. Almost always, I feel like I can't keep up, that I've lost the beat.

I'm always just slightly off. I worry that in my hurry to catch up with it, I'll trip and hurt my knee.

How do you measure the things that fill up the emptiness of the word enough? The love that overflows the roundness of the letter "o" or the soaring heights of a lowercase "h." It's a great, giant hole, the word *enough*. Stop the clocks so I can try to fill it, to shovel some shit into the vastness of it, fasten some planks across its breadth to walk across it, or at least to avoid falling into its great, giant nothingness.

It is bottomless, *enough*, and I am afraid that too much of my time is spent peering over the edge of the word itself, trying to see how far down it actually goes.

When I am less panicky and less anxious, I tell myself that if I am lucky enough to survive to the age my father was when those lumps and bumps got big enough to stop his heart, I will be able to catch my breath. The doomsday clock that is running in my head will stop its tick-tock echo. Maybe a new one will start, but perhaps in that moment between the two, there will be a lifetime of room, as if the clocks had actually stopped and every moment after will feel like a gift from beyond the grave, stolen time that I can burnish and polish.

Maybe I am overthinking it all. Maybe it's just time, after all, that fills the well of enough, just seconds and minutes and hours and days and months gluing themselves together until it's solid enough to keep you from falling into the darkness.

I'd like to think that each moment after sixty would be delicious, illicit in a donuts-and-wine-for-breakfast kind of way. More likely is that those moments would feel normal. There would still be dinners to cook and hugs to give and bills to pay. There would be sunlight to feel on my skin and raindrops that patter on the windowpane. The march toward the end would continue apace, the heartbeat drumming faster and faster and faster until it couldn't keep up with itself and stopped, until I set my weary bones down on the pavement and exited the parade for good.

Or perhaps it's the other way around. Maybe all of those moments will slow until the stretches in between grow so long that you're not aware of the clocks stopping. Not at all.

And in that last tick—long enough to hold a lifetime played backward in one last flutter of an eyelid—will be everyone you ever loved telling you yes.

It was enough.

when i'm an old woman

. . .

When I'm an old woman, I will use the fanciest moisturizer I can buy—the thick, creamy kind that comes in pretty jars. I won't ration it. I won't save it for a rainy day or try to make it last. No, I will slather and lather and baste myself like a holiday goose. I will crook and scallop my fingers to spoon it out in syrupy dollops, the way I once spooned chocolate frosting from the can my mother kept in the fridge.

When I'm an old woman, I'll put chocolate frosting back on my weekly shopping list, and when the clock strikes twelve, I'll eat it straight from the can, letting pools of sugar melt in the center of my tongue.

Forgive me, it was delicious, I will say to the cat.

When I'm an old woman, I will spray pricey perfume on my wrists when I have no plans other than reading novels on subway cars traveling north. I will anoint myself with holy eau de toilette, and when random strangers wrinkle their noses, I will tell them to kick rocks.

When I'm an old woman, I will eat every piece of birthday cake given to me. I'll smash it into my mouth until angel-food crumbs fall from my grin. I will lick lurid buttercream roses until my teeth are the color of a Caribbean sky, my tongue as blue as Smurfette.

When I'm an old woman, I'll start a petition to abolish tiny suffixes tacked onto words—all those Smurfs and only one Smurfette!—nothing but caboose syllables that scream *afterthought*. I am the perfumed freight train! I am the supple-skinned goose course! I am the marquee event—no marchioness for me, thank you not at all. And the people who file such petitions will mutter and say *she is mad!* But no matter. I will be old, and I will not care one whit-ette or fig-ess.

When I'm an old woman, I will sit at green felt tables and play poker with men. When they offer pretty things to the young woman serving them drinks, I will put my gnarly hand over hers.

They never ask you to go all in, I'll say. But trust me, you'll keep betting half an ounce of soul-flesh every hand. Then life will see you, and then life will raise you until one day you wake up and there's hardly enough soul-flesh left to fashion a self.

I will tip her chin toward me and tell her how much work it takes to rebuild a self when you've sold your soul to the ideas of men. I was young once, I'll tell her. I know.

Then I will flip the table over and walk out in a cloud of fancy perfume funk.

When I'm an old woman, I won't worry about the back of my hair or lipstick caking in the corners of my mouth. I'll spend those hours tap dancing instead. I will spit out anything diet, low-fat, or lite. I will gaze at my naked body in full-length mirrors and write poetry to my knees, to my hips, to the belly that once carried life.

Odes and couplets and sonnets dedicated to the body that stuck by me, despite how I raged against it.

How do I love thee? I will sob because when I'm an old woman, I'll wish I had known how to be kinder to myself.

When I'm an old woman, I'll smile less and snarl more,

baring what teeth I have left instead of folding myself into something nice and unobjectionable like an origami swan.

Swans are vicious enough to cut a bitch, you know.

I will walk with my elbows out and refuse to yield sidewalk inches and spread my knees on rumbling train cars and plant my forearm on the shared armrest of middle airplane seats, daring anyone to object. I shall be more objectionable, not less.

When I'm an old woman, I'll drag a box to the public square and stand upon it to speak truths.

The world devours the dreams of girls; it chews them up and spits them back into their laps, mushy and unrecognizable, and

No matter how you speak or look, it will never be enough or it will be too much, and there is no in-between—not even a razor edge to balance on and

"She was selfless" is an obituary line for women whose families never knew them at all.

When I'm an old woman, I'll wear shoes with a boxy toe and throw away all my pointy heels. I will unbind and uncurl my piggies and luxuriate in wide-width footwear with a solid arch. I'll take a class to learn how to create the perfect smoky eye. I'll wear sequins and leopard print and feathers and armfuls of bracelets so heavy they would drown me if I stepped into a lake.

I won't, of course. Step into a lake, I mean.

When I'm an old woman, I'll surround myself with other old women, a post-menopausal posse, a grandma gang, a congregation of crones. We'll roam city streets in packs, like men. We'll link arms, elbows out, and hiss like ancient swans. We'll hide cans of frosting in our shopping bags and eat from them when we tire.

Who are those women? They will say when they see us, *the ones that smell like the ghosts of girls past, the ones with such glowing, supple skin, with sugar-sweet chocolate staining their lips?*

We are your daughters and sisters; we will sing and snarl and howl. *Your mothers and grandmothers, your fantasies and nightmares. We are all the things you told us we couldn't be.*

When I'm an old woman, I will tell every girl who hugs my knees not to wait until she is old. I'll offer my frosting to sweeten bitter truths.

But I was young once.

I know they won't listen.

dearly beloved

. . .

DEARLY BELOVED
WE ARE GATHERED HERE TODAY
TO GET THROUGH THIS THING CALLED MIDLIFE
UPSIDE DOWN TIME, THIS MIDLIFE
IT FEELS LIKE FOREVER, AND THAT'S A
MIGHTY LONG TIME—
BUT I'M HERE TO TELL YOU THERE'S
SOMETHING AFTER MENOPAUSE
A WORLD OF MODERATED TEMPERATURE
WHERE IT DOESN'T FEEL
LIKE THE SURFACE OF THE SUN
BOTH DAY & NIGHT

if you can't stand the heat

. . .

We love to poke fun at menopausal women.

Middle-aged women shoving their faces in the freezer or fanning themselves with whatever is handy—it's comedy gold. Even women laugh at it, or at least young women do.

That's because no woman in the history of womankind ever *thinks* she's going to be old enough to feel like her skin is melting off her bones.

Oh, it's all fun and games while the estrogen floweth from the hormonal tap, when the boobs are perky and skin is supple. Alas, perimenopause will get you, my pretty, and your little dog too—and by your little dog, I mean the hairy Italian Nonna 'stache you're going to sprout on your upper lip.

It happens to the best of us.

Out of all the symptoms that define the change—what a quaint word, change, like you're swapping out the throw pillows —the one most people are familiar with is the hot flash.

I can only speak of my own experiences, but...you can't prepare for a hot flash. I can write twenty thousand words about what it's like, and to be honest, I probably have, but it's something you need to feel for yourself. Some women, I've heard, feel a little warm, and that's the end of it. Others need to have a change of clothing with them when they soak through the linen shift dress they wore to work.

Lucky for you all that one of my superpowers is baring my experiences on the altar of embarrassment so that someone else knows what to expect.

First tip: Hot flashes are not created equal. Nor are they always flashes. Flash sounds quick and snappy, like a hot little number you can jazz hand your way through. Shuffle ball change and done! Not so.

Not even close.

So, for your guidance, here's a mini field guide to hot flashes.

The slow burn

This is the one you can feel coming on, barreling toward you like a freight train holding the molten core of the earth itself. It builds and builds until—like a summer storm-- it finally breaks, spreading rapidly from your core to the tips of your fingers. Often this happens when you're standing with someone you've just met. Or your boss. Or someone you're trying to impress. You might try to surreptitiously fan yourself with the back of your hand. Don't bother. It does nothing. If you're lucky, you'll have time to excuse yourself and get thee to the nearest open door. Otherwise, you may look *and* feel like the Wicked Witch of the West melting into the floor.

The Devil's Breath

The spontaneous combustion-type hot flash that comes out of nowhere. WHAM! One minute you're sitting watching Netflix under your headphones, happily temperate, and the next you are literally tearing layers off because if your socks touch you

FOR ONE MORE SECOND, YOU ARE GOING TO DIE. The Devil's Breath causes some amusement among other family members. Depending on where you are in your hormonal journey, you may either laugh along or start googling *how not to throat punch your loved ones during perimenopause.*

The Marriage Killer

The one that led me to refer to my beloved spouse as a *human flesh blanket*. You're cozy in bed, and then your spouse inches closer to you. You test the waters. Hmmm...ok. They inch closer. Still ok. Yay! And then, at the point of contact, a finger touching the ridge of a vertebra, a toenail grazing a calf, it's like the sun bore a hole in you. Like space lasers pierced your home. The blankets fly off. The door is flung open. Your spouse accuses you of things like witchcraft and skulduggery.

The Panic Attack

The mother of all flashes. Trapped inside your own solar flare, you panic and wonder if anyone has actually died because they've cooked from the inside out. Your body is a greenhouse in the middle of the Mojave. Internal organs are close to the boiling point; you are a human sous vide. You might experience intense claustrophobia, not just regular fun claustrophobia, but the feeling of needing to escape your own skin because it is on too tight. No one is coming to save you.

The Flashette

You feel a little flush and brace yourself to run to the nearest available freezer, but it fizzles like a wet sparkler. A minor dab of the forehead with a silk hanky would take care of it. It's all very demure, very mindful. A quick fan of the hand and an upward blow under the hairline, and you're good to go. The Flashette is sometimes followed by comments like *Huh. I'm not sure why everyone complains about this!* Or alternatively, *looking back, the whole thing wasn't so bad*. Lies, all.

The Climate Change

A sudden onset hot flash, maybe a slow burn or a devil's breath, which is immediately followed by feverish chills as the air dries your sweaty body. Lather, rinse, repeat. If your body had an on-air meteorologist, they'd have whiplash. You cycle through endless rapid-fire highs and lows, leading you to invest in a wardrobe consisting of cardigans and tank tops that can be layered, and anything that can be taken off and put back on with ease.

The Night Terror

As the name suggests, this flash is not really as much of a flash as an REM-interrupting heat wave that prevents you and your partner from getting any sleep. The one that led my husband to muse about sponge pajamas. This ebb and flow of heat leaves you tossing, turning, and understanding why Europeans are fans of the two-duvet system. Night sweats? More like night soaks. The sheets are damp, your hair looks like you've gotten out of the shower, and no one is getting any sleep.

I wish I could tell you that it'll all be over in a flash, but that would be a lie. It's a jungle out there, folks, and not just the swampy temperatures it feels like inside your jeans.

Forewarned is forearmed, or perhaps I should say fore-warmed? One day you'll be able to wear a sweater again, I promise.

THINGS I THINK ABOUT WHEN I'M TRYING TO SLEEP..

The name of the kid who got a paper clip stuck
up his nose in 2nd grade...

Did I take my pill?

Kick-ass responses to mean things someone
said in 8th grade...

Whatever happened to Craig of the Blond Hair?

I wonder if I'm in anyone else's vacation
photos?

.What would happen if I forgot to take my pill?

Did I return that dish, or did it move with us?

I wonder how many carrots I've peeled...

.What would happen if I took two pills?

What was Mr. S's last name, anyway?

Did I fill out that form?

Did I turn the oven off?

Did I take my pill?

dream works

. . .

S ometimes, the things that keep me up at night are intrusive thoughts like "Are we on the brink of WWIII?" Other times, I'm up on melancholy hill worrying that my kids didn't have movies like *E.T.* or *The Goonies* to dream along with, but instead movies based on video games, Marvel superheroes, and a live-action Dora the Explorer. Don't get me wrong, I like Thor as much as the next middle-aged cis-het mom, but I fret it's not the same.

Kids need movies about kids who are wild and free and regularly outsmart their parents. Kids need movies where they color outside the lines.

One year, during an '80s movie nostalgia fest with our kids, we watched *War Games*. I thought they would be confused by the size of the computers and laugh at the password on a post-it in the drawer trick. But what really threw them for a loop was the freedom that Matthew Broderick and Ally Sheedy had to navigate the world. As they boarded planes and traveled across the country, my kids, who like most of their peers had had their lives managed and Google Spreadsheet-ed to the minute, were flabbergasted.

Don't their parents know where they are? They demanded of us.

Life was different in the '80s, we shrugged. Less structured. More feral. Maybe you couldn't get on a plane and travel across the country, but you could ride your bike to the next town over, crossing a two-lane highway, and no one was the wiser. Maybe you couldn't set out for a two-day hike down the railway tracks to look for a dead body without someone wondering why you didn't show up for dinner—well, no, actually, you probably could do that.

Yet, all of that makes it even more perplexing to think that the generation who grew up with keys around our necks, frying Steak-ums and microwaving Hot Pockets with zero adult supervision, whose childhoods took place in a fug of second-hand smoke and insect repellent, turned into parents who track, monitor, and schedule our kids to the point of suffocation.

You'd think that if we have decided not to let them just be kids who can play a game of tractor chicken, build a woman in their bedroom lab, or travel through time in a phone booth, we'd at least give them movies where they can.

I hope they forgive us.

if i knew you were leaving, i'd have baked a cake

. . .

No one told me that as an adult, cake was expected at regular intervals.

I'm not a cake woman. My teeth have always been salty as opposed to sweet—even as a kid, dreams of sugar plums didn't dance in my head. I can skip dessert, pass up the pie, and just say no to the Oreos, but put a bowl of pretzel sticks in front of me and I'm a goner.

As a child, I wasn't interested in cooking or baking. Not even undercooked muffins baked under a 100-watt bulb in a Holly Hobby oven could tempt me into domesticity.

I skipped high school Home Ec and dragged my mistrust of kitchen gadgets with me into adulthood. Baking, in particular, perplexed me. Why bake a cake when you can buy one, or better yet, buy a bag of pretzels?

Once, I baked a birthday cake for an ex-boyfriend, perhaps trying to speak a vanilla-essence love language. His love language was booze, and in the end, it was all a bit of a mess. Party guests nibbled politely around the burnt bits, and I wasn't too offended when, later, I swept through the apartment and found paper plates piled high with picked-over slices.

I fell in love with a different man whose love language was not booze or, thankfully, cake, cookie, or pie. Life trundled along until we found ourselves docked in early parenthood, and our weekends morphed from brunch in Greenpoint to kiddie birthday parties at the soft play place.

I knew that eventually, I'd have to reciprocate and provide some sort of sweet treat, and truly, how hard could it be to make a batch of cupcakes for a herd of two-year-olds? It wasn't rocket science—or even baking soda science. I swallowed my hesitancy, my pride, and a few lungfuls of boxed cake mix and made a batch of cupcakes.

This time, there weren't nearly as many plates with napkins covering the uneaten bits like tiny cake shrouds.

More than anything, the act of making cupcakes for my son and his friends took a tiny Holly Hobby-sized bite out of the stigma I carried with me from childhood, the one about cooking and womanly domestication.

Kids'll do that, I've learned—soften your cold heart in ways you weren't expecting.

For them?

I bake.

We had another son. We moved abroad, and suddenly, I was a housewife well and truly, missing only the Kitchen Bitch T-shirt.

And then? Then I got bored. Like many women of my generation, women who thought they'd be chairing industry boards and not mopping floorboards, I was determined that if I was going to do the domestic goddess thing, I was going to take it to the next level. And so I started baking from scratch. I read recipes, sifted flour, converted oven temperatures, and started to churn out some decent cakes.

Then I bumped that up a notch. I started shaping cakes like

I used to shape my eyebrows in the '90s. I baked a cake in the shape of a dog. I made Lego bricks. A triumph of an R2-D2 cake. A dump truck and later a fire engine with licorice coil wheels. I decorated Lego Ninjago cakes, mummies, and a hole-in-one cake for my husband's 40th, complete with a fondant golf ball dimpled with a straw. None of these cakes were winning prizes, but they tasted good, and most importantly, they were made with something approaching love. By me.

Not quite a love language, but maybe a fondant sentence?

Over the years, my family's cake preferences were written in a book I carry in my heart. Vanilla cake with chocolate frosting for the oldest, chocolate with no frosting for my younger, and carrot cake with cream cheese frosting for my husband. And so the years sped by in an array of birthday cakes, every one of them made with love. By me.

Until recently.

MY OLDER SON'S October birthday sits squarely in school semesters and university terms. After our most recent move, he turned eighteen before our shipment with the cake tins and frosting tips arrived, and so a stack of store-bought donuts had to suffice.

The following year, he'd just started university, and it was our first birthday without him.

No recounting, in gory detail, the bloody details of his dramatic birth. No wishing him a happy birthday as soon as he woke up. Whereas once I used to scoop up his little body and shower him with sloppy mama kisses, that day I waited until a reasonable time—noon—to text him metaphorical mama kisses.

The next year was much the same. Off he went to university in another country and another time zone. Instead of ice cream for breakfast, we sent a card in the mail. In lieu of a new Lego set, we transferred money directly into his account so he could buy what he wanted. And instead of showering him with love, I waited for him to give me a time window to call.

The morning of his birthday rolled around, and my phone pinged with a text from him. It was a photo of a birthday cake, made with love.

By someone else.

"Look at the cake Isobel made for me," he wrote. "With buttercream! It's gorgeous!"

And it *was* a lovely cake, complete with a birthday message spelled out in those tiny candy letters I was always too cheap to buy, including his *name*.

Aw, sweet, I texted back. And then he dashed off because *Isobel—not me*—was making him pancakes or something equally nice.

I...well, look, I'm not ashamed to admit that it was not my most enlightened moment. I was not prepared for the complex feelings that followed that exchange.

I showed the photo to my husband.

"It's nice, no?" He asked, "That she made him a cake?"

"Yes, yes," I waved my hands around.

"So what's the issue?" he asked.

The issue?

The issue is that there was another woman who cared for my son enough to make him a birthday cake. *Was that not obvious?*

As my husband reminded me, despite all the caking and the making I've done, I don't actually enjoy baking. There's always a lot of washing up to do, the cocoa powder is a bitch to clean, and after one disaster, I live with a low-level fear of mixing up the baking soda and the baking powder.

None of that mattered in that moment.

I baked not because I loved doing it, but because I love my kids, I love my husband, and it made them feel special in a buttercream-sweet way. Maybe they didn't have dreams of sugar plums dancing in their heads, but they might have had dreams of Mom's cakes.

The act of baking for me was the equivalent of candy letters spelling out *"See how much I love you?"*

At that moment, I was unprepared for someone else to take on that role. It all seemed too soon, too fast. Life is a highway, and the exit signs were blurring by so quickly I couldn't read what they said.

"I have...big feelings," I said to my husband, possibly with the teeniest, tiniest hint of a tremble in my voice. "Making birthday cakes has always been my job. It's a mom's job."

"Oh God," I thought as soon as I said the words out loud. Am I one of those mothers?

I NEVER THOUGHT of myself as the kind of mother who dreaded the inevitable transfer of big feelings from me, the parent, to someone else, the partner. As my boys grew, I missed the chunky toddler hugs, sure, and sure, in the back of my mind, I knew that as they grew, there was a good chance those squishy boy hugs around my neck would transform into solid man hugs around someone else's. And truly, if my son was dipping his toe into the choppy sea of relationships, to do so with someone who cares enough about him to make him a cake—with buttercream? What more could I ask for?

Still, it was one of those strange threshold moments when it felt like I was crossing definitively from one side to another.

I was no longer calling all the shots, choosing the shapes and flavors, or in charge of the special things that showed my son love. The day's events, the exciting news and funny stories, the jokes, the little traditions. There's someone else who he cares enough about to share those things with, someone else who cares enough about him to share back.

Of course, it's a good thing, but these moments sometimes

take a little time to settle. Like flour dust on the counter. Not like cocoa powder, though, because remember—it's a bitch to clean.

THERE HAVE BEEN other moments in my life in which small, unexpected things have had a big, outsized impact. Sometimes, they slowly creep up on me, and sometimes, they wallop me over the head like an errant cake tin. It's not always the anniversaries or bolded-out days; sometimes it's randomness.

Once, my husband found me hiccuping with sobs when packing up the Matchbox cars. Another time, I found myself sitting cross-legged on the floor rereading the board books that had defined so many childhood nights.

Goodnight comb and goodnight brush, indeed. Now I was the old lady whispering hush.

On the day of the great cake transfer, I had felt a little sad about not being with my son, but it was a normal kind of sadness about the passage of time, of both of us getting older, of him being away from home more and more until soon, home would not be with us but somewhere else.

The cake, though.

The cake threw me for an emotional loop, like a roller coaster that pitches you upside down before you are suddenly upright once again.

I knew I was being ridiculous. I poked fun at myself by texting my boy mamas, who I knew would understand. They did exactly the right thing and sat with me in mock outrage. How dare she? They joked. But I knew they understood; they, too, are navigating these moments of parenting young adults who are making their own way in the world.

And how lucky my son is to have found someone who will painstakingly spell out "Happy Birthday" and his name in candy letters.

I hope that they treat each other's hearts with the same care.

IN THE FUTURE, maybe there'll be a time when he's home on a birthday weekend and I'll bake him a cake, for old time's sake, but it doesn't matter because from now on, I'll no longer be the only one. There will be others who care about him enough to do that, to take on the icing mantle.

Handing your child's emotions and heart to another person is...tricky. It's hard in those moments of change not to feel a little left out, a little sad, and a little nostalgic for the days when he would throw his arms around my neck and hold tight.

When we said goodnight to the moon and the old lady whispering hush together.

There are other necks to hug and other faces to cover with kisses, hopefully less sloppily. There are other ears to whisper into. There is someone else sitting across from him at the end of the day. This is, of course, exactly what you hope will happen. It's what the whole parenting malarky is about: to fluff their feathers and send them soaring into the world, to teach them a love language they can speak with someone else.

I just wasn't expecting that it would be a birthday cake that made me feel how empty his little corner of the nest already is.

fade to pink

. . .

A few years ago, when my children were little and summertime was for hanging out at Camp Nonna, my mother—the Nonna in question—was getting ready to go to lunch with friends. She stood in front of me, smoothing her top over her stomach and hips, and asked if she looked all right.

She looked *fine,* if by "fine," you mean perfectly, perfunctorily adequate, but mostly, eh.

"Come on," I said, walking over to her closet. I pulled out a hot-pink blouse that I'd never seen before. We dug out some chunky, turquoise jewelry and a pair of strappy sandals, and voilà. She had recently let her hair grow out to a beautiful silvery white, and it looked gorgeous against that pop of pink.

"It's not too...*much*?" she asked.

"Screw it, Ma," I said to her. "You're old. Now's not the time to fade into the background."

I wasn't saying it to appease her; I really meant it. Why should we hide behind beige and boring as we get older? She smiled and then, in an act reminiscent of my kids, spilled something down the front of her blouse.

Luckily, we found a sunshine yellow top to take its place.

IT SEEMS that women are expected, after a certain age, to gently fade into the background without muss or fuss. Somewhere between childbearing age and death, we're expected to gracefully make room for the next generation of young women who are, presumably, peacocking and preening in order to attract a mate. We are gently and not so gently encouraged to fade into our surroundings, blending in with the wallpaper until we're hardly noticeable at all.

Nah.

I shall not fade gently into that good wall. No, thanks.

Don't misconstrue. I have no desire, intention, or even capability of attracting attention of the sexual kind. Far from it. When out in a mixed-age social crowd, I've realized *with relief* that I'm of an age where I could legitimately *be the mother of some of the young men around me*—and not like a young mom either. Far from filling me with dread, I feel a tremendous sense of freedom, a burden that's flown the coop with my muscle tone and ability to stand without sounding like I stepped onto a sheet of bubble wrap. But just because I'm not interested in attracting sexual attention doesn't mean I am going to suddenly embrace ecru and speak in dulcet tones.

The older I get, the louder I get; in volume, opinion, and color. When I was in my forties, a swath of hot pink began to creep into my lifestyle. My cell phone was pink. My first Danish bike was bright, hot pink. When I was forty-five, instead of letting my hair fade to gray, I dyed chunks of it hot pink, something I never had the courage to do when I was younger and worried about other things.

I spent so many years as a girl and young woman running from pink and frilly. Because internalized misogyny is a thing, and disdain and mistrust of femininity run deep—as they were intended to do. Pink was for frivolous, non-serious people, and I was anything but non-serious. I had things to do and places to go and big dreams to make come true.

No, pink was for other people, other things, or so I thought.

THE CONCEPT of pink has been around for some time. In ancient Greece, it was a color for nature, not togas—the fingers of dawn were tinged with it. For a long time, boys wore pink because it was seen as a diluted tone of red, a color long considered masculine because of its association with military uniforms.

The radical feminization of pink didn't happen until after WWII, when the world was busy shoving women off the factory floors and into suburban kitchens. Suddenly, women in advertisements were dressed in frills and color, while men's clothing became simple, neutral, and, no doubt, full of pockets. And then, in 1953, Mamie Eisenhower wore a pink dress as part of her inaugural look, and the damage was well and truly done. Suddenly, the color was no longer associated with the rosy fingers of dawn or even with togas but with names like Mamie and words like "ladylike."

It was a pink line in the sand. You were girly and ladylike—or you rejected those things as frivolous and unserious.

Somewhere between the feminization of pink and the late '70s-early '80s push to reclaim the color as a form of rebellion—think The Sex Pistols—or activism—like the pink triangles used in LGBTQ+ activism—I was born.

Hot pink is not an ultra-feminine color, nor is it soft. It's kind of in your face. I've lived long enough to realize I am not ultra-feminine, though I gleefully embrace many aspects of femininity. I'm not particularly soft either (unless it's orphans; then I'm *marshmallow* soft).

I *can definitely be* in your face, though.

You don't need to drown in a hot pink sea or demand blue

streaks in your hair; the important thing is that no one should feel the need to hide themselves away just because they're over thirty.

Getting older doesn't mean you must fade away until you blend into the concrete.

I don't know about you, but I have a lot left to do and say.

So go ahead and buy the sequins if you love them. Buy the sparkle. Buy the hot pink sequin top that you'll never wear but brings you joy to see hanging among your other clothes. My own clothes get increasingly more colorful each year. Buy the stilettos or the mini-skirt. Buy the bikini and the screaming orange scarf. Swathe yourself in color. Dye your hair fuchsia. Or don't. Do what makes you feel good, not what some market researcher tells you you should be doing because of an arbitrary number of candles on your cake. And whatever you do, eat the cake.

In a world that expects middle-aged women to cede their spot in the line of life, don't be afraid to call attention to yourself. Don't buy into the fact that after a certain age, we have nothing left to offer. Don't fade into the background. Sing, dance, and wear bright colors. *Live.*

WHEN MY MOTHER came home from her lunch, still in her yellow top, chunky turquoise jewelry, and strappy sandals, I asked if anyone said, *Patty, you're too much.*

"Oh, you wouldn't believe how many compliments I got!" She beamed.

At eighty, my mother's got plenty of brightness left.

At fifty-something, I'm just starting to realize how much I have.

Screw fading to gray, I'm fading to pink.

life in joan collins mode

. . .

I started shaving my legs when I was twelve. That's how old I was when I finally convinced my mother to let me do something about the dark, downy hair on my legs, the matted forest of which made it look like I was smuggling a Yeti anytime I wore nylons.

Pantyhose? I can't remember what we used to call them; it's been too long. Only that the fancy ones came in an egg.

It's enough to say that I've been scraping the hair from my shins with a too-blunt razor for a long time, all the way until a year or two ago, when I stopped.

I didn't stop shaving because it's an outdated patriarchal notion—though it totally is—I stopped shaving my legs because when I looked down at my bare legs, there was no hair to see. I thought that I had reached the magical time of life I've heard about, the happily-ever-hairless age when your body fur grows sparse enough that there's no longer a need to shave.

For a dark-haired girl who used to have to shave her gams every summer day, it was a cause for celebration.

Huzzah!

Then, one day, I happened to have my glasses on when I

looked down at my legs. The hair on my legs had not stopped growing; I just couldn't see.

I took my glasses off.

I don't think it's a coincidence that around the same time that the wrinkles and neck sag start, your eyesight starts to go. Maybe it's Mother Nature's way of gently easing us into the second half of our lives. And truly, as long as you don't put your magnifiers on, it's a bit like living in a Joan Collins soft filter mode. Yes, the text on your phone is blurry unless you increase the font to "see-from-space" size, as my thankless children tease, and yes, you risk ordering borscht instead of a burger, but as long as you can't focus on the details, you probably look great.

Your eyebrows look plucked, your blackheads banished, your legs Yeti-less, and honestly, the turkey neck's really not that bad.

Without my glasses, I look great, at least ten years younger. All my friends, too. We're all rocking it, all the way into our fifties and beyond. Who would have thought we'd all look so good?

Without our glasses, anyway.

old wives card

. . .

When I got my Old Wives card in the mail
before I put it in my wallet,
the colorful one I got from a tourist shop
in a Barcelona alleyway
I held it in my palm
to show my husband

I'm an Old Wife now
I said
harridan and hag
my bones are made of superstition
and my blood sings with tales
I'm an old lady stitched together with folklore
a witch in the wood
not by the hairs of my chinny, chin chin

Come and tell me what ails you,
I said,
for I have the gift of sight

and he said well then,
can you tell me what are we having for dinner?
and so I turned him into swine
like Circe with Odysseus's men
who landed upon her island
and made a horrible mess of it all

Getting this card wasn't easy, you know
I said to the piglet at my ankles
who stared up in confusion, tail twitching
you think that Hercules had tasks?
Or Jason or Theseus?
Pffft

I am an old wife now with the card to prove it
softer in places
& harder in others
I have cardigans and a pair
of sensible shoes for walking
I'm not the woman you married

The piglet listened so carefully
and nodded so thoughtfully
that I changed him back
as I tucked my card away
for safekeeping
to show at the door
of the Old Wive's club

I'm not the woman you married
I said to my husband
as I buttoned my cardigan
and tied the laces of
my sensible shoes

I'm better

I know, he said
and then suggested
that we go out for dinner

interlude

Thirty springs have bloomed
Still I lay the stupid sheet
The wrong way around

———————

chasing waterfalls

. . .

My God, middle age is a magic-less time, an era of seriousness and financial planning, of joint replacements and retirement calculations.

Okay, I'm exaggerating a little—and also, you should have been planning for your retirement long before middle age—but it does seem like these middling years are defined by seriousness rather than silliness. There is magic here and there, but no one is pulling it out of a hat. It's something you have to seek out, rifling in unused coat pockets for a golden ticket or shining a flashlight into cupboards looking for genie jars full of whimsy.

When you're a seasoned adult, the magic of what is possible is no longer just there, waiting to be plucked like a harp string. Who's got time for that when there are bedsheets to change and salaries to earn?

Do you remember when you were eleven, maybe twelve, and you suddenly realized that it was deeply uncool to be excited about anything? Overnight, jumping up and down with anticipation or glee was replaced by eye rolling and shrugs.

Yeah, and? Whatever.

I remember wanting to imitate the older teens and adults

around me, the ones who seemed apathetic and jaded, unexcited by the things that used to thrill me. Everyone was so busy with life, with boyfriends and insurance premiums, oil changes and furniture polish, to believe in childish things like shooting stars.

It's another of those life thresholds I talk about incessantly, the moment when you step backward out of Narnia and close the wardrobe door on make-believe and magic.

Childhood magic wasn't simply the belief in fairies and Santa Claus, though; it was all the potential held in a summer day, the promise of after-school hours. It was deciding to go and chase a waterfall just because you could, even if it wasn't real.

As adults, we have to carve out time to chase dreams and claw back minutes to indulge in whimsy. A vacation. Between 3 and 4 pm on a rainy Sunday afternoon. A mental health day spent eating bags of chips under a blanket with *Bring It On* playing on the laptop. They all count, of course, but it's not the same as waking up on that first day of school vacation knowing that you had the whole summer to just be, when the most pressing issue was whose pool you were going to swim in and what you were going to do if Jenny ate the last blue raspberry ice pop. When the day could take you anywhere or nowhere or half a where in between.

When my oldest son turned eighteen, I half-joked that it was all downhill from there. "Peak hairline time of life," I told him. "Starting now, everything starts to recede."

He looked at me with such horror that I had to backtrack and promise I was just kidding, though part of me was serious.

What I didn't tell him was that I remember the feeling of wanting to rush through it all, to fast-forward to the good stuff —without realizing all those endless days, the belief in dreams, in bottle genies, and dandelion wishes? That *was* the good stuff.

Adulthood is soul-crushing sometimes. My days are filled with paperwork and lines and work and chores and bills and endless conversations about what to have for dinner. Always the dinner.

No one told me about the endless conversations about dinner.

My teen years were too emotionally tumultuous to want to return to, especially those early teen years when you don't know, from one day to the next, what body you're going to wake up in. It's like *Freaky Friday* if *Freaky Friday* was really Freaky Monday through Sunday and went on for several years.

But childhood, when make-believe reigned, when you could put a towel on your head and marry your best friend on the front lawn or put a clutch of weeds in a jar and marvel at their beauty? When anything seemed possible and no one was asking you what was for dinner?

I'd like to vacation there.

SOMETIMES, I end up lost in research that has nothing to do with what I'm writing. A path of random stepping stones that leads me to little islands of information, where I tromp around in wonderment until it's time to drag myself back to the shoreline of real life. Internet atolls, like the one I stumbled upon about children with past life memories.

These are children who recall vivid and detailed memories from a life they haven't led. The phenomenon has been studied and documented for decades, though there's no science to explain it. The accounts are jarring. Small children, some of them toddlers, who start to speak with a different tone or accent, who have a vocabulary beyond their years, who know names and dates and descriptions of things and places they would not ordinarily be able to know.

It's easy to dismiss it all as an imaginary friend or even a flight of parental fancy. Some believe it's parents leading their kids down a false memory path. The cynics among us, or even those looking for a rational, logical explanation, might think it's a way for parents to make a quick TikTok million or stake an umbrella in their fifteen-minute plot in the spotlight. Most parents, however, are hesitant to talk about it, fearful that they and their children will be ostracized, ridiculed, or harassed.

The borrowed memories almost unilaterally stop by school age, when the echoes go quiet. It's likely preoccupation; those growing brains are sorting through an influx of new information, navigating school, friendships, tasks, and a world outside of the imagination.

Most of the children never remember the things and places they spoke about or the people they recognized or swore they knew; the memories are simply gone, fading from scream to whisper, whisper to silence.

When you're a child, it's easy to believe in monsters under the bed and ghosts in the closet. Those things seem as possible as anything else, as possible as stars in the sky and faraway planets. Or zebras, which truly do seem impossible. As we get older, time starts to inch the door to that suspension of disbelief closed. Adolescence comes along and locks it. And adulthood?

Adulthood walls it up, paints the brick, and pretends there was never anything there at all.

Nothing to see here. Move along.

As GIRLS, my sister and I used to drag two wooden sawhorses that we called Snickers and Milky Way into the backyard. In a shady corner, under the big oak tree, there was a shed my father built. We'd throw open the doors to the mustiness of it, a home to spiders and rakes, a weed whacker encrusted with bits of lawn, and the winter saucer sleds. The plywood floor was slightly raised, and we would clear enough space for two lawn chairs to use as wagon seats. One of us would loop a rope around one end of Snickers, or maybe it was Milky Way, and suddenly we had reins to guide our trusty steeds over mountains and through amber waves of grain.

In those moments, we weren't just two girls; we were pioneers, taming the wilds of our imagination.

On rainy days, we'd gather with friends in our basement and play school or house. We'd teach a row of stuffed animals how to borrow or carry numbers, or walk around with an old check-book and busted cigarette lighter, mimicking the adults we saw around us.

The bathtub faucet was a waterfall for my Barbies to stand under. The rock wall in the woods was the boundary of a king-dom. Trees were ship masts for pirates to scour the horizon for treasure islands.

It's almost impossible for me to imagine such a time now, when a cardboard box could send you into space and a neigh-bor's pool was the Atlantic Ocean, which you could sail across over weeks and days, coming home in time for supper.

The memories of those things are there, but they're flat and two-dimensional. Echoes. The belief that made them come alive, even if they were only alive in my imagination, is gone. The colors and the details have been forgotten, pushed aside to make room for new things.

They're memories of a past life—not someone else's, but my own.

Sometimes, I catch a whiff of it when I get lost in a book or a television show, when I forget who and where I am for a few minutes. Sometimes, I write so furiously and for so long that it's like prolonged submersion. When I come up for air, right before I settle into the here and now, there's half a heartbeat when the impossible seems possible, a whisper of what it felt like to embrace the unknown.

. . .

PSYCHOLOGISTS ARE careful to point out that there's nothing to prove that these ghost memories are real—yet, they remind us, there is nothing to disprove them either.

It's the idea of the unknown that's so difficult for adults to grasp, I think, of trying to make something without form fit into a recognizable shape. We long to sort it all into spreadsheet cells and neatly cataloged boxes.

As children, though, we were comfortable sitting with the unknown, playing March Hare and inviting it to tea. The idea of a place or a thing that we didn't quite understand didn't seem to bother us as much. We simply accepted it, like we accept the reality of zebras.

Grown up, we spend a tremendous amount of time trying to name and tame the unknown, reminding ourselves that wishes don't come true because a star fell out of the sky—in fact, it's not even falling, I can hear you say. Or that past lives can't be real because the neurons in our brains stop firing when our hearts stop beating. No, it must be something else, something known.

We wall up the unknown and forget about it, our days and minds taken up by serious adult things, retirement things, and dinner things, until one day, you're writing an essay that takes you down a rabbit hole. When you emerge, pulling bits of leaf crumb from your hair, you swear you can hear the rush of a waterfall in that half a heartbeat, the half-beat where magic lives.

Before it closes up once again.

schlemiel! schlimazel! hasenpfeffer incorporated!

. . .

After school and before supper, I used to plop onto a beanbag and watch *The Brady Bunch* and *The Monkees* on Channel 56, WLIV, one of the two channels on the lower television dial. Remember the lower dial? On top of the television was a set of rabbit ear antennae with tin foil hats that twisted up. You needed to get them exactly right to get the picture straight. Sometimes a neon stripe bisected the screen, and if a wiggle of the knob didn't fix it, you watched anyway, tilting your head and pretending it wasn't there.

On Sundays, I listened to Casey Kasem's Top 40 countdown in the car on the way to or from somewhere, music crackling from the FM dial, poltergeist static between the stations. You could spend an awful lot of time fiddling and finessing those dials, and the wrong twist of the knob meant it was gone forever. You'd never get it back.

My mother's green Torino had locks you pushed down with the meat of your fist, and my '77 Chevy Malibu had windows that cranked open with a handle. Backseats were for stretched-out sleeping, there were cigarette lighters with orange ember glows, and ashtrays that clicked open and shut, open and shut.

I watched *Dirty Dancing* with my friends in a dark movie theater with a box of Junior Mints and a bag of smuggled popcorn. When I saw *Commando*, it was with the quarterback, and we held hands, our palms slick with teenage lust.

In high school, I, like, totally used the same catchphrases as my classmates, dude. We all had gravity-defying hairstyles, cemented in place with globs of Dippity Do and choking clouds of hairspray. God, the hairstyles. The hairspray.

The girls all smelled like Love's Baby Soft mixed with Wintergreen Life Savers with a slight whiff of Pall Mall. The boys of wood shop, gym class, and Irish Spring soap.

Commercial jingles for chewing gum and bologna embedded themselves into the recesses of our brains, where they continue to live like musical vampires, immortal. So kiss a little longer, stay close a little longer. I love to eat it every day, and if you ask me what I'll say...

We might have grown up in different places over a span of time. Some rich; most not. City mice and town mice. Racial and gender divides. Political ones. But all those things! Strands of our generational DNA—the Gen X Jordache genes that I have in common with the girl who had the locker next to me, or the boy from the next town over, the kids in the next state, or even a lad I hadn't met yet in a country across the sea.

They are the context clues we use to place each other on a generation timeline. Where were you when the Challenger space shuttle exploded or the Trade Centers came tumbling down? Do you remember Freddie Mercury at Live Aid, or when Fonzie jumped the shark? How many Luft balloons and what color were they? What day of the week was manic, who shot JR, how many licks to the center of a Tootsie Pop, and can you tell me what happens if you mess with the bull, young man?

They're the scratch-n-sniff words written on a Gen X membership card, the one you keep tucked behind the one for Costco and your driver's license.

How can those things not bind us together with Elmer's glue and giant tubs of kindergarten paste? How can they not shape who we are a little bit, like Play-Doh molds? All those shared memories that chlorinate our Wrangler gene pool.

Not wholly or irrevocably, of course; we're all individuals. More like the faint hint of light that remains when you unplug your Lite-Brite from the wall, or the outline of a painting that remains, even after you erase the lines, only visible when you hold the paper to the sun.

THINGS MY HUSBAND ASKS ME...

Where have I seen this actor before?
When is (fill in the blank)?
Where is (fill in the blank)?
What is (fill in the blank)?
What's the name of (fill in the blank)?

What are we having for dinner?

....

I meant, should we go out for dinner??

julestjerner

. . .

When I was a teen, a former classmate died in an accident. The shock of it reverberated through the neighborhood—most of us didn't know anyone our age who had died, and the sudden finality was jarring. A boy who'd sat at the same elementary desks and who'd drunk the same red and white cartons of milk was gone. We weren't friends, just two people that occupied the same childhood spaces, yet even now, at fifty-five, there are things I remember about him. The white blond of his hair, a small scar he had from a snowball that caught him above the lip.

That I remember those small things speaks to the way that a sudden death sears certain details into your memory, hot, sharp, and fast—like a branding iron.

He was there. And then he wasn't; the space he had occupied was a void.

Negative space has always been difficult for me—I'm not very imaginative in that regard. I don't think in visuals or spatial planes. It's hard for me to conjure up or imagine things or people that are no longer here.

What's left instead are holes in the shape of the person or

thing that is missing. Outlines punched through the fabric separating then and now.

Strange things happen when you try to make sense of negative space. An elevator lurches and makes you think of a time when someone jumped up and down, even though you'd asked them not to. The lilt of a stranger's accent, the way someone's mouth turns up, a jangle of keys, a turn of phrase, a song, an errant snowball, a coffee shop with wrought iron tables lined up in the sun.

I use these things to fill the holes left behind.

"IF I DIE," I said to my husband once, after a funeral, "I want you to invite everyone we know. Tell them to wear sequins and hot pink, to don their best leopard print. Tell them to wail and keen like a Greek chorus and write odes to their love for me on the backs of cocktail napkins."

"Really?" he asked, suspicious.

"No, do whatever you need to do," I said. "How am I going to know if they wore sequins? I won't be there."

To my friends, I said, "If I'm sick, I want you all to come and surround me while I'm still here. A final slumber party. We'll eat greasy pizza and drink gallons of Coca-Cola. We'll have to pee all night, but in between, you can tell me how much you love me. Bring me gifts of fruit and books and things that smell like the sea."

I miss the sea terribly.

"Really?" they asked, and I said, "Sure, why not? Surround me with love."

Reminders of loss do that sometimes, make you think about unspeakable, unthinkable things.

Then again, I'm a planner.

Everyone handles this stuff in their own way. Some people go quiet; others lash out. Some cry, some settle like a stone into their grief, immovable.

Everyone handles loss, or even the idea of loss, differently. You navigate down a river you don't have a map for, hoping you don't crash on the rocks and smash yourself to smithereens. If you're lucky, there are others in the boat with you to tell you to duck before you slam into a wall of shale.

SOME LOSSES AREN'T AS fraught or permanent. I live in a world of moving boxes and relocations, a revolving door of families and friendships. People come and go; families stay and leave. Goodbyes are as much a part of my everyday life as translator apps and passport renewals. You find ways to cope with the constant sense of loss—teas with frosted cakes and flutes of champagne, small gifts of remembrance tied with ribbons and bows, things to remind you of a certain time and place, of a certain group of people. And then you're gone, or they're gone, and somewhere, someone is left trying to fill all that negative space.

You promise to go back. They promise to come back. Sometimes they do; sometimes things happen that prevent either one.

I've never been good with negative space.

BEFORE SHE MOVED, my friend Juliette gave each woman in our friend group a hardback journal in jewel tones with our names embossed in gold and silver. Above our names was the name of the chat group we used to trade messages for years, first about our children, but then later, just for us.

It was a small testament to a friendship, of time spent watching boys grow into men, marveling at the way their bones seemed to stretch toward the sky. The aura of their friendship had expanded, engulfing us all; first outward to the mothers, then swallowing whole families.

The notebook sits on my desk in a new city, unused. It's too pretty, too special, and I have trouble deciding which words are deserving of such a gift. Which thoughts are worthy? Which sentences are special enough to capture forever between the covers?

What if I get it wrong? What if I waste those pristine pages on mundane things?

If I fill it with odes to love, with songs of people and place, what happens when the pages are full? Will it get packed away and brought out on special occasions and holidays, like the box of Christmas decorations in our basement?

Better, then, if it stays on my desk, the spine forever straight, the pages eternally white. Just as it was when she gave it to me, a time capsule—a way to transport myself back to a specific time and a specific place that remains unchanged.

There are other things I keep, bits and pieces of a life, mementos that act like remembrance stones that I can rub between my finger and thumb. On my bookshelf, there is a tiny bird, blue with an orange-feathered tail that leaves glitter on my fingertips whenever I handle it. There are books, earrings, a note-card from my father that lives between the pages of an old diary.

When it comes to gifts, I'm not the most thoughtful of friends. I'm not great with small tokens of appreciation. I tend to use words instead, even though they're harder to wrap. They all serve the same purpose, though; the twigs and leaves we use to feather friendships.

How do you measure a friendship? Is it in days or the length of time that you've known someone? Is it the number of shared experiences or how many times you've gossiped over cups of coffee, faces tilted toward the sun like wildflowers? Is it agreeing to crazy plans that have you stuffing a hundred bagels with cream cheese or dangling from a ladder to drape twisted ribbons of crepe paper from the eaves?

Is it the gifts you give or receive—a notebook, a tiny feathered bird, an exquisite birthday card, or a folded Christmas star in a crinkly cellophane bag?

MY FRIEND TALIA once told me about a group of friends from a time before I knew her, the ways they'd bonded over kids and carpool schedules, weaving their lives together—until the group was torn apart by loss. The bonds didn't hold, the friendship unraveled, and what had been a source of comfort turned into something else.

When loss tears through life, when it tears through bonds and friendships, how can it not leave negative space in its wake?

It leaves holes that you have to fill.

I TRY to be a good friend, though I'm not always sure what that means. The parameters aren't the same as they were when I was in kindergarten, when the rules were easier to understand. Take turns. Share your crayons. Don't throw a snowball that has a rock in it.

It gets more complicated when you're an adult.

There are times when a friend asks something of you, something wholly reasonable, wholly understandable, something that, by agreeing, means hurting someone else.

How do you weigh one against the other? Which is more important, whose feelings matter more?

There were things left unsettled in my friendship with the other recipients of those jewel-tone journals, those who were left. Things that scratched at my conscience, chafing.

I've never been good with negative space. There were holes that needed filling.

WHEN WE DECIDED TO MEET, Juliette and I had already moved from the city we'd all called home, and so we traveled back to the place where we had celebrated the ends of school years on breezy beaches with pizza and wine.

While I was there, Monica and I went for walks in the damp woods and along the sea.

I miss the sea terribly.

We met up with Lizzy and Ineke, and we walked under heavy gray skies that somehow felt perfectly, exactly right. We sat around Ineke's table, and her husband brought us food that he'd graciously made before he left us alone. Lizzy brought a bottle of wine she'd found with the name of our old group chat.

We ate and drank. We talked. We cried. We remembered. We laughed more than we expected to.

Juliette disappeared and came back with strips of sparkly paper, and I groaned because I was the only one left at that table who knew how to make Julestjerner, woven Christmas stars.

There should have been six at the table, but there were only five.

I read from a photograph on my phone of a piece of paper I'd hastily scribbled instructions on years before. Words that had made sense at the time but now just seemed to be a mashup of random arrows and verbs. Even with my glasses, it was hard to make out what I'd meant.

"Over, under, fold, now *through*!" I kept imploring.

"No, not that through, the other *through*!"

Lizzy and Monica were doubled over in laughter. Ineke poured more wine.

I walked around the table like a kindergarten teacher,

praising their folding skills, unfolding, and demonstrating when I could.

Over, under, through. Weave, flip, fold, turn.

Paper strips are flimsy things; they tear easily. If you make your creases too sharp, you can't reuse them if you make a mistake and have to start over. You have to be gentle.

When you weave them together, though? You get something more formidable, something stronger, something that lasts.

They might have been a bit mangled, a little clumsy, but that night, we all left Ineke's table with a star clutched in our palms.

NOT LONG AFTER OUR REUNION, I pulled our box of Christmas decorations out of storage. I searched, but I couldn't find what I was looking for. There were dozens of Julestjerner I'd made over the years, but I was looking for the ones that had been given to me by someone else, the ones that had come in crinkly cellophane bags, larger than the rest, strung on a length of velvet ribbon.

I used to hang them from knobs and a set of decorative antlers above the fireplace.

I looked in the hatboxes where I stash the decorations that I inevitably forget to put away every year, stray ornaments, and baubles. I sat on the floor, surrounded by broken bits of old clay ornaments, sticky shards of candy cane glued to my fingertips. It's possible that in the chaos of moving, the stars got lost. More likely is that when we were deciding what to keep and what to take, I reasoned that in the end, they were only paper stars.

Whatever the reason, they were gone.

I WENT to the art store in the mall near my apartment and bought strips of glossy red and white paper and another packet of silvery shimmer that looks like windowpane frost. I went to another shop and bought cellophane bags. I pulled out my note-book scrap of scribbled instructions and sat down.

Over, under, through. Fold and weave. I made a lot of mistakes at first; I always do, trying to carefully unfold and smooth those fragile strips to fold again. My back ached, but in front of me, I had a growing pile of Christmas stars.

A few days later, a group of women, new friends in a new city, came for brunch. I told them stories of the place I used to live, of Juliette and Monica, Ineke and Lizzy. I told them how we'd changed the name of our group chat because it was too hard to see the old name flash up. I told them how just a few weeks before, I'd walked around the city with them, a small bird pinned to my coat, how it left glitter on my fingertips whenever I touched it. Of how we'd sat, carefully folding fragile strips of paper into something lasting. Julestjerner.

When my guests left that day, I handed each of them a small transparent bag to take home. Nestled in each was a red and white star.

I'M at an age now where loss, no matter how sharp, is something you keep half an eye out for. It's no longer the unexpected shock of a grade school classmate. Now, it's the friend who did the makeup for my wedding, the wife of my husband's childhood mate. The barflies who sat next to me on stools in a Second Avenue bar. Acquaintances I hear about on social media. Dear friends who haunt my thoughts when I least expect it.

Paper strips that wove through my life in one way or another.

IF LOSS TEARS through and takes me in its wake, bury me in the pink sequined shirt that's hanging in my closet, the one I've never worn. Lay my head on my leopard print robe. Surround me with books and fruit and things that smell of the sea.

I miss the sea terribly.

On my desk is the notebook Juliette gave me. Open it and write all the words I worried weren't important enough.

In the sideboard is a packet of shimmery paper strips. In the top drawer of my desk, there is a narrow piece of paper with hastily scribbled instructions. L to R, over, R to L, through. Flip. Fold.

It will be hard to follow, but I trust you to figure it out.

Punch a hole in the top and string it with ribbon. Carefully place it in a cellophane bag and give it to someone else. Tell them all the ways that others have woven themselves into your life, fragile strips that together make something strong.

Something beautiful.

tales from a middle-age marriage

. . .

A long time ago, whenever my husband went on a business trip, he would come home with a piece of jewelry. Nothing particularly fancy or expensive, just something he'd seen that he thought I would like.

When my jewelry collection threatened to engulf us in Murano glass, he switched to cosmetics that I would never buy for myself because they were too expensive. For a time, my foundation was Chanel.

When I stopped wearing makeup, he switched to the fancy moisturizer that I'm too cheap to buy for myself, the one that smells like mangoes and is supposed to firm up your skin.

Lately, he's had to travel more than usual, so I'm stocked up on moisturizer, but the last time he went away, he came home with the eye cream I use, the one that, even though it's a little on the pricey side, I *do* buy for myself because after all these years, I decided certain things are worth the money, like the bags under my eyes.

"Oh! I was just about to run out of this!" I said to him in surprise when he handed it to me.

"I know. I looked to see what you might need before I left," he said.

Relationships aren't about buying jewelry or a fancy foundation or even moisturizer that smells like summertime and is supposed to tighten the jiggly skin on your ass; they're about paying attention to what your partner needs, even if it's just eye cream.

IT'S NEVER JUST eye cream.

nostalgia is a
gateway drug

. . .

In a Danish supermarket, an abandoned toy in an empty fruit crate once triggered a poignant longing for long-ago sandbox days. It was like a dopamine hit to the soul. I thought of chunky little fists clutching toy cars and those Mama-centric days when I was all they needed. A flood of memories was jarred loose by the sight of that little black and yellow digger.

It happens. A random sight or sound, a phrase or a song, the spine of a book a stranger on a train is reading, and your brain starts to play a round of Go Fish, looking for a memory to match.

Oh, look! A small toy like the ones we used to bring to the playground. Brain, do you have any memories? And your brain scrolls until it finds a match—the feeling of sand running through your fingers, your toddler's chicklet-tooth smile, the way the freckles dotted their noses like cinnamon dust.

A toy digger abandoned in a supermarket is an occasional thing, like hearing Simple Minds on the radio or a postcard that falls from between the pages of a book that you pluck from a shelf. You might get a quick hit of nostalgia, a flush of warmth in your veins, like the first sip of creamy cocoa on a snowy day.

Those things are occasional and organic, unlike the memories foisted on me by social media, those daily tech reminders that encourage me to go back in time, whether I want to or not. When I do click on them, I'm often confronted with how much time has passed. How has it been a decade since this happened? How has it been eight years since that vacation, five years since the pandemic, and on and on. They're there, waiting for you every day or every week. Click on me, click on me.

Technology has found a way to hook us on nostalgia. And nostalgia?

Nostalgia is a gateway drug.

EVERYWHERE I LOOK, there are nostalgia peddlers, pushing those misty memories on me. High-waisted jeans, for God's sake. Thick-soled Reeboks. Rick Astley and Axl Rose. Commercials selling insurance with songs from The Cure, secondary characters from the movies I grew up with who have their own television shows, reboots, remakes, and reunions. Fuller House.

We're micro-dosing nostalgia on a daily basis.

Ah, but where's the harm? Is anything other than your unvacuumed rug going to suffer if you spend half an hour excavating photographs to find the jawline you used to have? If dinners go uncooked because you spent an afternoon rereading love letters from the last century, is anyone going to get hurt?

Just one more letter, one more photo album, and one more trip down memory lane. I can stop anytime I want!

The danger is getting stuck in the past, forgetting the whole truth in favor of the highlight reel. When you spend too long reliving the past, it's easy to gloss over the fact that those days of yore were never as good as you remember, at least not wholly.

. . .

I AM no stranger to excavating the past, descending deep into the nostalgia mines, a flashlight in my hand, clamped as tightly as a digger in a toddler fist. I wander through tunnels and peer into crevices, shining my beam in wide arcs to see what I can find.

The glints of gold that pick up the light are easy to spot.

What I remember most about growing up in the '70s and '80s was the sense that anything was possible. A static charge of change hung in the air like heat lightning. Girls could climb trees! We could wear pants, play sports, and go into space. We could wear sneakers with suits that had shoulder pads the width of a doorway. Singing "Free to Be You and Me" at the top of my second-grade lungs made me certain that if Willy wanted a doll, there was no good reason why Willy should not have a doll. Get the boy a doll, for goodness sake!

When I'm digging around in the past, my light beam catches the sheen of that possibility, the sense that we were getting somewhere, that we were moving on up. Maybe not to a deluxe apartment in the sky, but forward and upward. Clare Huxtable was a new kind of role model, Rhoda was single, and Molly Ringwald was out there proving in film after film that the quirky girls could bag the hot guy.

Even if it was sometimes the wrong guy. Poor Duckie.

Even if the right guy traded his girlfriend like a baseball card to get there. Oh, Jake.

The light beam dims.

There was a whole lot wrong with the '70s and '80s, too, which is exactly why we have to be careful down there in those memory veins, huffing the past like glue.

IT'S EASY, when we're high on the good stuff, to forget just how problematic the good old days were. Trading your hot girlfriend to the geek in exchange for a pair of pilfered panties? We didn't blink. White actors in Blackface on a movie screen?

Didn't bat an eyelash. My father loved *Blazing Saddles*. I tried to watch it once and was so horrified at the language and the tropes that I had to turn it off after ten minutes. The same with *Trading Places*.

Oh, but if Richard Pryor was in it, or Eddie Murphy starred, we might justify it, without the context that Black actors and women actors often had to be thankful for the crumbs they were given, stereotyped or not.

"*That's just how it was back then*," I hear a lot. That may be, but it was just as wrong then as it is now.

I didn't have words for these things when I was growing up. No one taught me they were wrong. Handsy bosses have been pinching employee buttocks since the first boss chased his assistant around the Roman well, but back then, there was no name for sexual harassment. Racism was ever-present, but a lot of White people in the US were living high off the Civil Rights movement, pretending that everything was hunky-dory. Racism? What racism? Rosa Parks sat on the bus, and MLK, Jr. made a speech, and now everything's fixed! In my very White bubble, the dumb jokes were about blonde women and Polish immigrants; the insults were about Mexicans, Asians, Jews, and Blacks.

Queer adults and kids existed, of course, but few were open about their sexuality. AIDS was talked about like it was a punishing plague targeting gay men. As teenagers, we tossed the word "gay" around like confetti. I sometimes think of the students I sat with in the cafeteria, the ones who danced to the same high school soundtrack—those who later came out as queer. How hurtful it must have been to hear their lives reduced to one-liners and insults by people they considered friends.

It was wrong then, too; it's just that very few of us were taught to care.

This is the part where the flashlight you're holding blinks out and you're left in the dark.

Life was better when... Fill in the blank with the nostalgia flavor of your choice.

We all do it. I do it. I've done it in other essays in this collection, even, but living in and longing too hard for the past sometimes means stunting our chance at growth, at change, at progress. It means chasing down the good—or what we thought of as good—and ignoring all the icky stuff that sticks to the good like burrs. When we harken back to the *good old days*, we often forget that what was good for us came at the expense of others, for whom things were decidedly not good.

When I came across the little digger abandoned among the apples, it made me think of my boys, of a time when they were small enough to ride on my hip. I thought of the endless trips to the playground and the big plastic bag of trucks that came with us everywhere. It made me think of their squishy cheeks and the weight of their small bodies on my lap, heavy with sleep.

In other words, the good stuff, the warm and fuzzy stuff. If my brain ticked through my memories and told me to Go Fish, I might draw the card that reminded me that when they were little, no one slept. Or the tantrums that seem to be part and parcel of toddlerdom. Or the long, monotonous days. Another card might remind me of the exhaustion. Or I might pull the top card off the memory deck to be reminded of the times I spent wondering what had happened to the girl who sang about Willy wanting a doll, the one who dreamed big dreams that did not include spending her days making truck noises in a sand pit.

No one likes to remember the hard times, the bad times, or the sad times, but they were there too, running right alongside the warm, cocoa-flavored stuff.

But you can't see those when the flashlight blinks out.

We all miss–people, places, times, and things. I miss my twenty-something breasts. I'm sure my husband does too. It's natural sometimes to feel a bit maudlin when you think about those days of yore. There's nothing wrong with clicking through your vacation photos from ten years ago and remembering what a great time you had, or hearing a song and remembering the scent of a boy's neck when you danced in the dark.

Be careful out there, though. They know what they're doing, those nostalgia pushers, a little vacation photo here, a birthday message there. Suddenly, life in the past seems nothing but rosy and sweet.

That's how they hook you.

First, it's a hit of nostalgia, but soon you find yourself needing more to keep you going until, the next thing you know, you're voting for folks who want to turn back the clock fifty years.

love letter to the body

. . .

I t should be easier to face a reflection in the mirror than it is to face the secrets of a soul, easier to bare a breast, a hip, an ankle than to see unmasked the wings and horns of a self.

And yet...

And yet...

And yet it almost never is.

Even after all this time and thought and searching and acceptance and writing, I maintain a complex relationship with my own body. This husk of muscle and flesh and spark and firework, this weight of tendon and sinew and bone and passion. This body.

We circle each other warily. Often, we are at war, waging battles against one another, laying siege. At times, we live under the flag of an uneasy truce. But the peace is always tenuous. There is always a new front to be claimed, another battle on the horizon.

This body.

These legs. These crepe-skinned knees and flesh-heavy thighs. These legs, which have carried me through five and a half decades, which have run me up mountains I thought too high to climb, which have scaled heights I thought impossible from where I stood looking up.

These arms. My God, these arms. These arms, which are baggy and saggy and on their way to bat-winged. These arms, which have cradled and rocked babies to sleep, protecting and soothing. These arms, which have carried the weight of what is needed to feed my family, which have wrapped around generations, pulling grief close, pulling joy closer.

These hands. Christ, these hands, which have woven the threads of love and passion and family together into a tapestry of life. These fingers, which fly clacking over keys and sometimes seem to know what I need to say before my own mind recognizes it.

This womb. This womb, that hollow source of heartache. This womb, which eventually harbored and nurtured two little lives, which had the strength to push those lives into this world to stand on their own, apart.

These breasts. No longer high and mighty, these forlorn breasts. These breasts, which nourished two sons, and these hips, always too wide, curved and rounded leftovers of my mother's body, which expanded to accommodate and grow new human beings.

This spine. This spine, just now starting to lean. This spine, which has stood upright in the face of change, of heartache, of sorrow and grief. This backbone, which has borne whatever I have heaped upon it without breaking, without complaint or crack.

This body. This body, which has starved itself and run itself ragged trying to fit a tortured and distorted ideal of its own making. This body, a safe haven for a lover to harbor in, warmth and depth in which to burrow. A lap in which to snuggle, flesh soft enough to absorb the sharpness around it.

This body, which despite all of this, still only loves itself part of the time.

This heart. This heart, which bears the scars of breaking, which has been pieced back together, and still beats in time with a love ferocious and fearless. This heart, which still has not completely learned to love what has loved me back so fiercely all this time.

This body.

interlude

Snap crackle and pop
Used to be for cereal
Now it's morning knees

———————

fifty-five candles

. . .

I was only thirteen when *Sixteen Candles* was released. To me, a tall, flat-chested teen who longed for boobs and a boyfriend—in that order—sixteen was a portal to a different dimension. Sixteen was the bridge between those awkward early teen years, full of angular limbs, braces, and stubborn baby chub, and *real* teenagerdom, when you could drive and date and walk down the hallway with your hands in each other's Levi's pockets.

Wishing on sixteen candles seemed like the first step into adulthood, into real life, and, of course, into relationships.

When we last saw Samantha Baker and Jake Ryan, they were sitting on a tabletop, shyly confessing their feelings to one another. Maybe their flirtation would have lasted a week or two and fizzled out like so many teenage crushes. Or maybe they would have stayed the course.

At sixteen, they probably would have been ready to speed into adulthood in that red Porsche of his, ready for all the fun and maybe even a little bit of the responsibility. Few of us have any real idea of the weight of that responsibility at sixteen or eighteen or twenty-one.

Samantha and Jake would be around my age by now. If they did stay together and kept that Porsche, I don't think their knees would let them climb in and out of it so easily.

It's a slow creep, adulthood, until you wake up and there aren't sixteen candles on your birthday cake, but fifty-five.

WHEN I WAS A KID, the stretch between birthdays seemed like an eon. A Paleolithic era could have fit into the twelve months in between those wishes. The school year stretched endlessly, and an entire lifetime could happen in the fifteen minutes before the final bell rang. Worlds began and ended in between locker slams and running for the bus.

Time was like taffy, stretched and elongated, in endless supply.

Then, without warning, time stops stretching so much and instead starts to snap back until one day something in your back snaps and you're left writhing on the floor thinking, "How did it all come to this?"

How did this happen so fast? How did it happen without me realizing? Was I simply asleep at the wheel? Not paying attention? Too busy playing Wordle?

Fifty used to seem ancient. Fifty was an age for old Italian ladies in thick-soled black shoes and knee-highs that barely contained their swollen ankles. It was white-haired men in newsboy caps and canes. Fifty was *old*.

Until you get there yourself.

No one tells you that, despite the increasing number of candles on your cake, in your mind, you're far younger.

Some days, I look in the mirror and see my father's mother staring back at me, and I have to turn away because sweet Jesus on a corn dog, wasn't it five minutes ago when I was just a girl, staring at Craig of the Blond Hair, praying that he'd notice me?

Was I not just mixing bad cocktails and celebrating turning twenty-one, toasting the endless expanse of time ahead of me?

Twenty-one! If my teens were for sneaking Bartles & James wine coolers down by the bridge with Diane, and my underage years were for drinking watered-down screwdrivers at the Scrap Bar, then twenty-one was for champagne. Or, at the very least, sparkling white wine. And then whoosh, there's a film montage set to "Eye of the Tiger," and you're a middle-aged mom of two, standing in front of the mirror, pulling your skin taut to see how it would look if you got a facelift. Not a full one, mind you, just one of those mini ones.

It turns out that time—the concept—has no correlation to time—the reality.

In my mid-fifties, I don't feel sixteen anymore, or even thirty-five. Forty-five seems to be about where my brain timed out and stopped counting candles.

SUPPOSE Sam and Jake stayed together. Maybe Samantha went on to college and studied marketing. Marketing was a hot major in the '80s. Maybe Jake started working in his father's business; whatever he was doing to finance that big house in the 'burbs must have been successful.

Samantha and Jake are young and in love, motivated to succeed and *go places*. They are made for one another. They get married—yes, mawwied–sheesh!—have two kids. Somewhere north of Chicago, they buy a modest suburban dwelling and settle into a comfortable existence. School runs and Little League, check-ups and Sunday dinners, Girl Scouts, Boy Scouts, gymnastics, ballet, T-ball, laundry, food shopping, changing the sheets, and comparing insurance quotes.

In other words, life.

. . .

SIXTEEN, the reality, was too *too*. Too intense, too extreme. Too full. There was no nuance; there were no gray areas at sixteen. A note passed under the desk had the potential to upend your week. A fight with your best friend, and it felt like your world was imploding. The news was AIDS and *Red Dawn*, nuclear armageddon, acid rain, acid wash, razor blades in your Halloween apples, and strychnine in the Tylenol.

If it was the end of the world as we knew it, I did not feel fine.

Still, there are times I miss the depth of those teenage feelings, the way they popped with neon color, orange and pink in your body. They were feelings that you could actually feel, in your bones and in your blood, sitting like a star cluster in your heart. Maybe it was because it was the first time you were feeling it. The double-time beat of your heart when a boy asked for your number, triple-time when he called. The way a breakup melted you from the inside out. The way you were absolutely, 100% sure it was the end of the world because your mom said you couldn't go to the Howard Jones concert with Kelly.

No nuance.

The math sends me spiraling sometimes. High school was nearly forty years ago. My husband and I have been together for nearly thirty years—we've hit that point in our relationship where we've known each other longer than we haven't. We've lived more of our lives together than apart.

It's a startling thing to wake up and recognize that statistically, you've got less time ahead of you than you do behind you. The stretch of road in the rearview mirror is long enough now that you can't see where you began, but there, in the not-so-distant distance, is the end of the road, figuratively and literally.

The fact that there's nothing that I can do to go backward, to throw my life in reverse and back up a few years, is hard for me to swallow sometimes. Oh, I can try and squeeze in a few extra exits by lifting weights in my dining room and taking the stairs more often. I can eat more plants and fewer animals and make sure I put sunscreen on, but that still does not change the fact that time is passing, more quickly than it should.

Time is no longer taffy. It's an elastic band stretched between my fingers, taut and ready to take my eye out.

GOOD FRIENDS once told us the story of the bottle of fancy champagne they were saving for a special occasion. The bottle languished in their fridge for weeks, then months, until they finally realized that the pressure of deciding what counts as a special occasion was just too much. So one random Tuesday, they had fish finger sandwiches and popped open the bottle.

At fifty-something, it's likely you've had the graduations and the marriages, divorces, and babies. Special starts to take on a different meaning. And maybe that's the trick to this whole game of life: changing your definition of special. Special becomes a Tuesday night when you have a bottle of fancy champagne in the fridge and you're together and no one is tired or has had a shitty day at work. Special is an unplanned movie night when everyone is home, the wind is howling outside, and you remembered to buy hot cocoa.

Maybe the problem with aging is that we keep chasing down our teenage or young adult definition of special. The butterflies from that first kiss. The feeling of handing in that final exam paper.

The first time someone leans over a birthday cake and wishes you a happy birthday.

IF I HAD to imagine what Samantha and Jake's middle-aged marriage looked like, I would guess that it would be like most of ours—highs and lows—but more often than not, endless calendar days where you chalk it up as a win if you are, to paraphrase my favorite Norwegian expression, up and not crying.

Perhaps Samantha's dreams of being a career mom died when the kids came so close together. Maybe it was an unpleasant and difficult death, leaving behind a ghost of resentment. Most of the time, the ghost stays buried under the dinners and school runs, but sometimes it rises up and clanks its chains, demanding to be heard. Maybe the pressure of taking over the family business weighs Jake down. Maybe he struggled with the heavy-duty responsibility of providing for a growing family. It's a far cry from the career he had dreamed of, far from his rich kid past when the economy was booming. The wheeling and the dealing are exhausting, the constant compromise and negotiation just to make a buck. But Sam and Jake ride the ups; they whitewater raft the downs. They are Samantha and Jake, ships that met in the night on a course bound for happily ever after. They go out to dinner every now and then. They host barbecues with burgers and beer in styrofoam coolers and fruit salad in a hollowed-out watermelon. Sometimes they go and see a movie.

Even Cinderella and Prince Charming have to deal with the minute and the muck, the monotonous and the mundane. Jake and Sam are no different.

Sam puts on a few pounds, and she dyes her grays. There are fine lines and wrinkles beginning to sprout: laugh lines and worry marks, the creases of time and motherhood, of love and loss. She buys one of those red light masks and a weighted vest. Jake sports a slight paunch that he can usually camouflage with a bit of care. He starts running half-marathons. They can't remember the last movie they saw in the theater.

The barbecues they used to host became less frequent when the divorces started. Sam doesn't like the second wives; they are too young, too pert, too...blank. There aren't many second husbands.

She has thought, more than once, that all the trading in for a new model is simply kicking the can down the road. The younger second wives will turn gray and softly padded with time, and then what? What happens when they, too, become old wives?

One day, Sam sees a picture that a friend has posted on Facebook and notices that Jake is starting to lose his hair. Jake Ryan is going bald. She hadn't noticed before. In between the food shopping and working and shuttling to and from ballet lessons, between the Saturday golf and the doctor's appointments and the bake sales and the Scout meetings and college applications. Between the meetings at the office and the piano recitals, they don't really see each other. They see each other, of course, peeking through a pile of folded towels, at the one or two dinners they have each week as a family. They see each other in photographs after the two-week vacation they take every year to the house on the lake. They see each other as they are passing the salt or spitting toothpaste into the sink.

It's been a long time since Samantha looked at him with the starry eyes of a young girl gazing up at the most popular boy in school. A lot of midnights have come and gone. She's outgrown glass slippers and bikini briefs and moved on to flats and Spanx. His belt has been loosened a few notches, and she sees now he really is starting to lose his hair.

But! In all the years of births and deaths, of loving and honoring, of rich and poor, of sickness and health, he has never once forgotten her birthday. There has always been cake; there have always been candles.

That counts for a lot, she knows.

Even when the number of candles is more than she wants to acknowledge.

THERE ARE days I look in the mirror and hardly recognize the woman staring back at me. Life has been turned down a few notches, the colors are softer, and the music of my youth is in episodes of Bridgerton. The sharp edges of those first kisses and flutters of sexual attraction are there, but not as serrated.

Is it any wonder that when we hit this mid-life range, a lot of us desperately seek something that gives us the flutters, the butterflies, and the intensity? It's the oldest cliché in the book.

Maybe it's not going back in time as much as going back in feeling.

The feeling of getting in a red Porsche without your knees cracking or your back spasming, taking off knowing there's a lot more open road ahead of you than behind.

WHAT IF THERE had been a sequel to *Sixteen Candles*?

Now in their fifties, Samantha and Jake decide to reconnect with each other by taking an empty nest road trip. They rent an RV because, let's be serious, at their age, comfort is way more important than coolness. While they're away, it's Sam's birthday, but Jake has already phoned ahead and ordered a cake to be delivered to the campsite they've booked. The RV fridge is stocked with wine coolers—he had to search for those—and beer and a single bottle of fancy champagne. There's a bag of fish fingers in the freezer. In the glove compartment is a map they dug out from a box somewhere, one of the old kinds that folds like an accordion. Sam found an ancient mixtape and got one of her kids to transfer the whole thing to a playlist. She puts it on, not too loud though, because it's hard to concentrate when the music is too loud.

After its endless tail, "Purple Rain" finally ends, and the opening chords of The Thompson Twins fill the RV.

Jake looks at Sam, and Sam looks at Jake, and they smile, laugh lines from a well-lived life crinkling around the corners of both their eyes.

"Where should we go?" Jake asks.

Sam thinks for a minute. "Let's see where the road takes us," she answers finally. "As long as I don't have to worry about what's for dinner, I'm happy."

And they drive, neither of them focused on what's behind them or even really what's in front.

The joy, they've learned, is in the journey itself.

THINGS NO ONE TOLD ME
ABOUT GETTING OLDER...

It's hard to hear when the light is too bright
Middle-aged love is like a warm bath
Adult kids are fun
Time works differently
Your Nana was right, prunes really do work
1995 will always be 10 years ago
You should have kept all your stuff because it
all comes back in style
Sunglasses hide a multitude of sins
Your knees go first
It really does go by fast
It's always the right time for champagne

don't you forget about us

Dear Mr. Vernon,

We accept the fact that somehow, our entire generation is middle-aged. But we think you're crazy for making us read an entire book of essays about who you think we are. The world sees us as they want to see us. Can you define an entire generation in simple terms or convenient definitions? Brainy Boomers, Princess Millennials, Basket Case Zs, and Alpha Athletes? Aren't we all a little bit of everything?

Psych!

Gen X is 2 good 2 be 4 gotten

Sincerely,
The Gen X Club

...us to deep freeze a ridiculous
amount of fat stores to get through these
events. So there we were, dumped at the
other end of menopause, carrying an extra
45 pounds, swaddling nothing, but resentment,
and longing for... years--perhaps

...uld have been cause... anticipation — but that was
...ent and anticipation — but that was
...long time ago, back when it seemed
...e something gossamer & nebulous,
...e the MILKY WAY — too far away to
...ontemplate, too far away to touch...
...ow that that time is closer, close enough
...see the cracks & crevices and the d...
...anger they pose to your balance, you
...st want to slow it down. But
...ith the space analogy it... rather than what you are
...u forward like a... supposed to do. Are commandments always
...es set tho... not supposed to do. Are commandments always
...written in the negative? Did I miss that

...supposed to do rather than what you are
...somewhere?

Don't wear miniskirts or long hair or trendy
clothes because then you might be taken for
mutton dressed as lambs and somehow we all
know how bad it is to be mutton who act...
...ing, for certain, what mutton actual...
...to look younger but not too...

I sha...

...to be ...
Kondoed, purged and culled and organi...
50 years of thoughts and ideas — you would
think the head is like an attic but right
now it feels more like a basement, crammed full
of half a lifetime's worth of unexpressed
emotion... and half-lived dreams shoved in
the co... Aunt Mary's china and
the cu... ...thirty years
ago. ... ...few
a n...
sent...
w...

It's true what they say about nostalgia —
being a gateway drug. Or at least I say it.
I'm the "they" I guess.
Not too long ago there was a meme about
"and that's how I ended up on the floor of
the kitchen surrounded by old photo albums a...
crying" and boy, did it feel like I was s...
How many times do you start by cleaning ou...
your closet and out of your pocket of a dress...
haven't worn in 10 years comes a ticket stub
and down the rabbit hole of memory you go a...
by the time you come back up its time t...
cook dinner and your closet is still unorga...
Alice in the looking glass only Alice is ...
as young as she used to be.
"Oh my, is that the time the restaurant...
brought the "wrong" meal and... no, it's the...
time the waiter spent 10 full minutes flourish...
the b... ...on the ... dumped ke...

thoughts from the
b side of a gen x life

This is a Love Song

A — Companion

Date _____
N.R. _____

We're Not Gonna Take It—Twisted Sister

Rio—Duran Duran

Be My Baby—The Ronettes

Purple Rain Soundtrack—Prince & The Revolution

Rumors—Fleetwood Mac

Old Time Rock n Roll—Bob Seger

Holding Out for a Hero—Bonnie Tyler

Crazy Train—Ozzy Osbourne

Radio Gaga—Queen

Crazy For You—Madonna

Playlist available on spotify

B — Playlist

Date _____
N.R. _____

Left to My Own Devices—Pet Shop Boys

Free to Be You and Me—Marlo Thomas & Friends

Pretty in Pink—The Psychedelic Furs

Saving All My Love For You—Whitney Houston

Keep on Lovin' You—REO Speedwagon

Islands in the Stream—Dolly Parton & Kenny Rogers

Total Eclipse of the Heart—Bonnie Tyler

Ball of Confusion—Love & Rockets

If You Were Here—Thompson Twins

Don't You Forget About Me—Simple Minds

playlist

This is a Love Song

Companion playlist

coda

In defense of the essay

When people ask what I do, my answer is "I write."

The answer is intentionally vague. I've written two books—well, three now, I suppose—yet I don't really think of myself as an author. I've published fiction and poetry and have two unpublished novels gathering dust, but I don't think of myself as a novelist or a poet.

So, yes, the answer is vague, but it's the most truthful approximation to what I feel I actually do.

I write.

Invariably, those two little words trigger a response. Sometimes from strangers or friends of friends. Once, a customs agent at a foreign immigration desk somewhere.

"A writer, eh? So, what do you write?"

Sometimes, it's genuine curiosity, but there are times the question is thrown like a gauntlet, flung down like a challenge.

Oh, you write, do you? Prove it. Quote Shakespearean sonnets from memory! Correctly spell onomatopoeia! Give me three instances where a semicolon is warranted. Speak pretty sentences all in a row!

As if, by identifying myself as someone who strings words

together for both a living and a loving, I must prove my bona fides.

Oh, I write, do I? What *do* I write?

I write shopping lists on scraps of paper that live in every pocket. I write sappy birthday cards that I keep in a shoebox in a cupboard just in case one day I need to remember how I felt about my husband in February 2002. I write curse-laden rants on social media. I write lunchbox notes and slam poetry that I perform in front of audiences. I write online reviews and song parodies. I write snippets of scenes of somethings in an array of notebooks I have stashed around my house. I write ideas. I write dreams. I write memoir, fiction, and haikus. I write articles and blog entries and emails to the bank.

That's a bit of a long-winded answer, even though it's the closest thing to the truth. In the aim of brevity, I've come across a more succinct answer, which has the benefit of being both true and getting people off my back.

I tell them I write essays.

I've noticed that when I answer, "I'm an essayist," the conversation stops in its tracks. *No one knows what to do with an essay.* Essays are the stuff of Mrs. Concannon's ninth-grade English class, of blue-book exam questions and book reports. Essays are for heavyweights. Important things are discussed in essays. Essays belong in *The New Yorker* and *The Economist*.

Of course, none of that is true. Essays are as varied as those who write them. Which makes me wonder why they aren't more popular, especially as we age and our eyesight goes and our attention span declines, but there are still a hundred different things pulling us north, south, east, and west. Maybe an essay is the perfect answer.

Doctor, I can't read for too long because it hurts my eyes, and frankly, I fall asleep. What's your prescription?

Essays!

Admittedly, I'm slightly biased, but I think essays are in dire need of a rebrand. Instead of being seen as the stuff of academic show-off-ness or elitist literary hors d'oeuvres tucked in the pages of periodicals, those of us who write essays should do more to talk up the versatility of the form.

Essays are the chocolate box of prose, small offerings that sometimes leave you with a lingering sweetness and other times make you pucker in distaste. They are an unexpected shaft of sunlight or a rogue raincloud breaking up a picture-book blue sky. You can read an essay over a cup of coffee or while you're waiting at the doctor's office to talk about your failing eyesight or where your sex drive went.

Truly, why aren't we all reading more essays?

Perhaps when people inevitably ask, "What do you write?" instead of using essays as a way to get them to leave me alone, I'll answer with gusto and panache, a Whitman's Sampler of topics in my bag.

"You should try one," I'll tell them, "they're delicious."

—DMH

liner notes

Acknowledgments

Thank you to the Pilgrim Village kids who played kick the can until the porch lights came on, who knew how to get to the fort in the woods, and who rode in endless circles around the block —you all season my memories in different ways.

Special thanks to the girls who shared their Aqua Net with me then and now: Diane, Joanne, and Kelly.

Thank you to my sister, Karen, the embodiment of childhood imagination and magic, who helped me guide Snickers and Milky Way through the plains and then grew up to design the cover of this book because she's awesome like that. Thank you, Mom, for, well—for everything, really. It's hard to know where to begin. Dad, wherever you are, thank you for teaching me what enough looks like.

Thank you to the Bonus Moms for always keeping me grounded, even when I'm upset about birthday cakes.

Thank you, Rup and Caroline, for sharing your champagne story, though I maintain that fish finger sandwiches are gross.

To Rowan and Reed—may you both keep a sprinkling of childhood magic in a pocket of your heart to pull out when you need it. Thank you for letting me tag along through your childhoods.

To the best of husbands, the best of men, who finds me when I'm lost—physically and emotionally. I love you to the 212th floor.

To my Berlin book club, some of whom graciously volunteered to read a nearly done version of this collection and provided much food for thought: Amulya, Sunny, Suzanne, Louisa, Shalini, Iza, Sara, and Pratima. Thank you.

None of this would have happened without Aqua Net, The Breakfast Club, and Love's Baby Soft; without Craig of the Blond Hair, Simon Le Bon, and Molly Ringwald. Finally, thank you to Prince & The Revolution for giving me the soundtrack not only to a book but to a generation.

Gen X 4eva.

words & lyrics

About the Author

Dina Honour is the author of *It's a Lot to Unpack* and *There's Some Place Like Home: Lessons From a Decade Abroad*, as well as hundreds of essays, thousands of lists, and two novels, which will likely never see the light of day.

She also writes excellent birthday cards.

Born and raised on the East Coast of the US, Dina currently lives with her family in Berlin, where she writes in the shadow of a former wall. Her work idles at the intersection of feminism, culture, relationships, and life abroad.

Meet her there, and she'll tell you a story.

Find out more at dinahonour.com, or sign up for author news at Word of Honour.

before you go

. . .

I hate asking readers to leave reviews.

Alas, here I am doing just that.

Small press and indie writers rely on reviews and recommendations to get their work in front of more eyes. If you've enjoyed what you've read—and I sincerely hope you have—then please help spread the word. Tell a friend and ask *them* to tell a friend. Ask your local library to order a copy. Get your book club involved—and if you do, get in touch; I'm happy to drop in for a conversation. Share links, sing my praises on social media, and yes, please consider leaving an honest review wherever you get your books.

Your eternally grateful author bestie,

Dina